An opinionated guide to

LONDON

Written by
EMMY WATTS

British Museum (no.29)

INFORMATION IS DEAD. LONG LIVE OPINION.

This book is totally useless. Everything you could possibly want to know about London is available for free via ChatGPT. Right?

Wrong! This book is not designed to give you endless information, it's designed to give you hard-won, well-distilled opinion. We're a small independent publisher and we live and breathe this glorious city. These are the places we'd send you to if you came and stayed on our couch. (It's not a very comfortable couch so perhaps get a hotel.)

Keep this precious book close: it may be the last bastion of human intelligence with which to shield yourself against the bright lights of a robot future. Alternatively, you can use it as a beer mat.

Martin
Hoxton Mini Press co-founder

MAKER
Someday
other
useums

Conservatory Archives (no.71)

Left: Design Museum (no.39)

ANY BUNCH
MEIJER
STOCK
Roses

Columbia Road Flower Market (no.70)

Marksman (no.20)
Right: The Pelican (no.84)

THE PELICAN

Hampstead Heath (no.41)

TIRED OF LONDON?

London: it's crowded, polluted, there's no air-con on the tube and the price of a pint is frankly ludicrous. And yet it's still one of the greatest, greenest, most beautiful places on the planet.

London is a melting pot. A glorious amalgamation of cultures and contradictions. A city filled with misfits, creatives and rebels. A square hole for square pegs. It's Mohican-haired punks in Camden Market. Spirited street performers in Covent Garden. It's the pulsating Notting Hill Carnival and Haggerston's annual clown church service. It's a gazillion things to nearly nine million people.

And while it's true you won't catch many Londoners talking a stranger's ear off on the tube (the badges encouraging small talk on the London Underground, predictably, did *not* go down well), you could hardly call us intolerant. When the British public voted to leave the EU in 2016, Greater London was the only region in England that voted to remain, leading to 180,000 Londoners petitioning Mayor Sadiq Khan to turn the capital into a sovereign city-state. Proudly multicultural, it's one of the most ethnically diverse cities in the world, with more than 300 languages spoken in a 25-mile radius and an astonishing 41 per cent of Londoners born outside the UK.

London's history is diverse, too – hardly surprising, given that there's nearly 2,000 years of it. The city has withstood plagues, the Great Fire, civil war, the Blitz. It's been the stomping ground of Shakespeare and the site of grisly royal antics, the birthplace of radical ideas and pioneering art. London's vast lifespan is evident in its collage of buildings: marvel at the splendour of Hampton Court Palace (no.33), at the domed masterpiece of St. Paul's (no.37) and the Barbican's Brutalist bulk (no.40). But perhaps the best way to experience the capital's history is to simply pull up a barstool at one of its copious pubs.

And while time stands still at some of London's better-known sites – such as century-old caff E. Pellicci (no.16), British dining institution St. JOHN (no.1) and Victorian department store Liberty (no.56) – the city as a whole is in a constant state of flux. In fact, London moves so fast that by the time you get round to reading this book, countless new places will have opened, with eateries, exhibition spaces, boutiques and bars popping up almost daily. But therein lies its charm. In a place as ephemeral as London, only someone tired of life could be truly bored (to paraphrase Samuel Johnson's well-known assessment).

Yes, London is a city built on tradition but, perhaps more significantly, it's one built on reinvention. Sure, we've got Beefeaters, Buckingham Palace and Big Ben, but you won't find those hackneyed cliches in this book. Instead, you'll find the places that people who live here actually frequent (including a fair few in Hackney). Not a tourist's guide, but a *Londoner's* guide.

Emmy Watts
London, 2024

A PERFECT WEEKEND

Friday night

Begin on a heavenly note: Evensong at St. Paul's (no.37). Cross the Thames in pursuit of global gastronomy at one of Borough Market's (no.17) many restaurants, then catch a comedy (or a tragedy) at Shakespeare's Globe (no.28) – or a late showing at the BFI (no.88).

Saturday morning

Fuel up with coffee and pastries at Jolene (no.22) before heading for Hampstead Heath (no.41) – perhaps via Conservatory Archives (no.71) if you'd prefer to bring the wilderness inside.

Saturday lunch

Linger over lunch at the majestic Sessions Arts Club (no.13), then proceed to homeware haven Pentreath & Hall (no.59) and stationery store Present & Correct (no.55) for some light browsing. Alternatively, make your way to Marylebone for proper sandwiches from Paul Rothe & Son (no.14) and a mooch around Daunt Books' (no.57) atmospheric galleries.

Saturday afternoon

Absorb an exhibition or two at the V&A (no.32), making time for tea and a scone in its historic cafe. Or hire a GoBoat (no.51) from Paddington and embark on a self-drive adventure along the Regent's Canal.

Saturday evening

Make an early-evening reservation for hidden hotspot Rochelle (no.19) before heading for wine and cocktails at Sager + Wilde (no.77) and dancing at MOTH Club (no.90).

Sunday brunch

Plunge into Sunday with a spot of wild swimming in Hyde Park's (no.49) iconic Serpentine Lido, followed by a leisurely brunch of Arabic French toast and za'atar Bloody Marys at Palestinian spot Akub (no.11). Or, if flowers are your thing, start east at Columbia Road Flower Market (no.70), ending up at E. Pellicci (no.16) for one of their famous fry-ups.

Sunday afternoon

Indulge in some architectural admiration (and perhaps an exhibition) at the Barbican (no.40) before meandering to Shoreditch for some independent shopping, courtesy of The Mercantile (no.66), Goodhood (no.69), Labour & Wait (no.62) and AIDA (no.63).

Sunday evening

Install yourself in one of the capital's finest gastropubs and while away the evening wining, dining and watching the world go by. Choose from Irish charm, live folk bands and Thai food at Skehans (no.82), memorable roasts (and an even more memorable ceiling) at The Audley (no.81) or pints and proper pub grub at The Pelican (no.84).

BEST FOR...

Outdoors

London has an astonishing 3,000 parks nestled inside the M25. Hampstead Heath's (no.41) spectacular skylines and swimming ponds, Kew Gardens' (no.44) tropical glasshouses and and Hyde Park's (no.49) contemporary galleries and historic palace should all be top of your list.

A rainy day

Don't let bad weather cloud your fun: make a dash for the Brutalist Barbican (no.40) for pioneering performing arts, Tate Modern (no.31) for awe-inspiring art or the British Museum (no.29) for a tour through two million years of human history.

Families

Battersea Park (no.47) is home to a children's zoo and one of the capital's largest playgrounds, while a self-drive GoBoat (no.51) seats the whole family. Young foodies will be wowed by BAO's (no.25) kid-sized portions of Taiwanese comfort food.

After dark

Hoof it to MOTH Club (no.90), for carefree club nights in kitsch surrounds, Wilton's (no.79) for theatrical delights in the world's oldest Grand Music Hall, the Faltering Full-back (no.83) for pints in an Ewok treehouse (no, really) and Drumsheds (no.89) for all-day dancing in a former IKEA.

On a budget

E. Pellicci (no.16), Paul Rothe & Son (no.14) and Beigel Bake (no.15) are all as beloved for their reasonable prices as their food, while Rio Cinema (no.87) offers cut-price tickets on selected days. St. Paul's (no.37) even hosts a free daily Evensong service.

Soaking up history

The capital heaves with history. The Globe (no.28), despite not being the original, will transport you to Shakespeare's London. Then there's Hampton Court (no.33), favoured palace of Henry VIII (and home of numerous historical spectres).

Retail therapy

Money burning a hole in your pocket? Fritter it wisely at one of London's eclectic indie boutiques. Gratify green fingers at Conservatory Archives (no.71) or hit up AIDA (no.63) and Couverture & The Garbstore (no.67) for hip threads. If you're feeling indecisive, head to Liberty (no.56) or Coal Drops Yard (no.68) for endless, irresistible choice.

Something different

If you like your attractions out of the ordinary, this is the city for you. A Bar with Shapes for a Name (no.86) proposes a wonderfully offbeat drinking experience, and you can't top concept dining spot Sketch (no.12) for an eccentric night out. Or perhaps bouldering in a Victorian pumping station (no.52) is more your cup of tea?

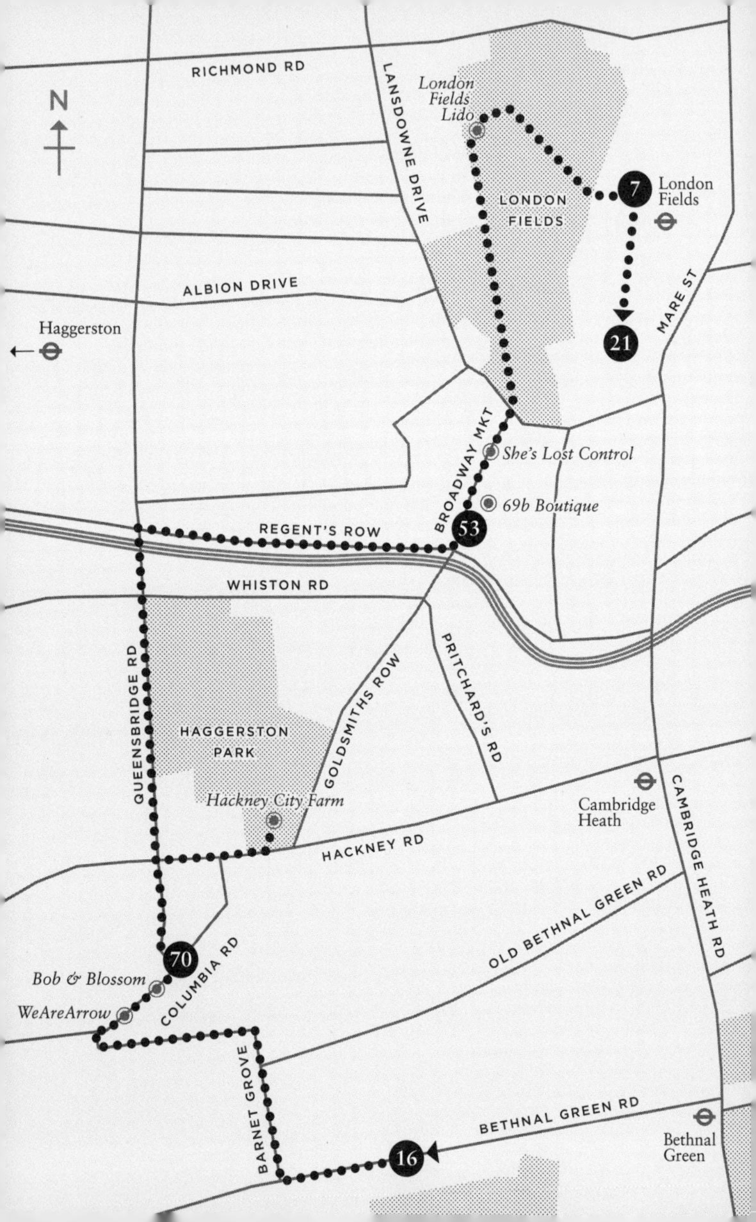
RICHMOND RD
N
LANSDOWNE DRIVE
London Fields Lido
7
London Fields
LONDON FIELDS
ALBION DRIVE
MARE ST
Haggerston
21
BROADWAY MKT
She's Lost Control
69b Boutique
53
REGENT'S ROW
WHISTON RD
PRITCHARD'S RD
GOLDSMITHS ROW
QUEENSBRIDGE RD
HAGGERSTON PARK
Hackney City Farm
Cambridge Heath
CAMBRIDGE HEATH RD
HACKNEY RD
OLD BETHNAL GREEN RD
70
COLUMBIA RD
Bob & Blossom
WeAreArrow
BARNET GROVE
BETHNAL GREEN RD
16
Bethnal Green

WALK 1

East London Sunday mooch: Bethnal Green to London Fields

Fuel up with a fry-up and some Cockney banter, courtesy of family-run institution E. Pellicci 16. Once your bubble and squeak's gone down, mosey over to Columbia Road 70 and bag yourself some blooms from its Sunday Flower Market before exploring its parade of colourful indie boutiques, working eastwards from *WeAreArrow** for ethical jewellery to *Bob & Blossom** for cute kidswear. Cross Hackney Road, swinging by *Hackney City Farm** to say hi to the ducks and donkeys. Carry on towards Broadway Market to continue pottering, hitting up Artwords 53 for design-led books, *69b Boutique** for sustainable womenswear and *She's Lost Control** for cloudy crystals and scented candles – not forgetting the Sunday stalls. Stroll through London Fields, stopping for a rest on the grass or – should you be feeling particularly energetic – dropping by the *Lido** for a few open-air laps. You've probably recovered your appetite by this point, so finish up with a fat sourdough sandwich at E5 Bakehouse 7 or grab a jam-packed pita from Pockets 21 and scoff it back in the park.

Walking time: 1 hour, 2.2 miles

Total time with stops: 3–4 hours

**Not in guidebook: more info online*

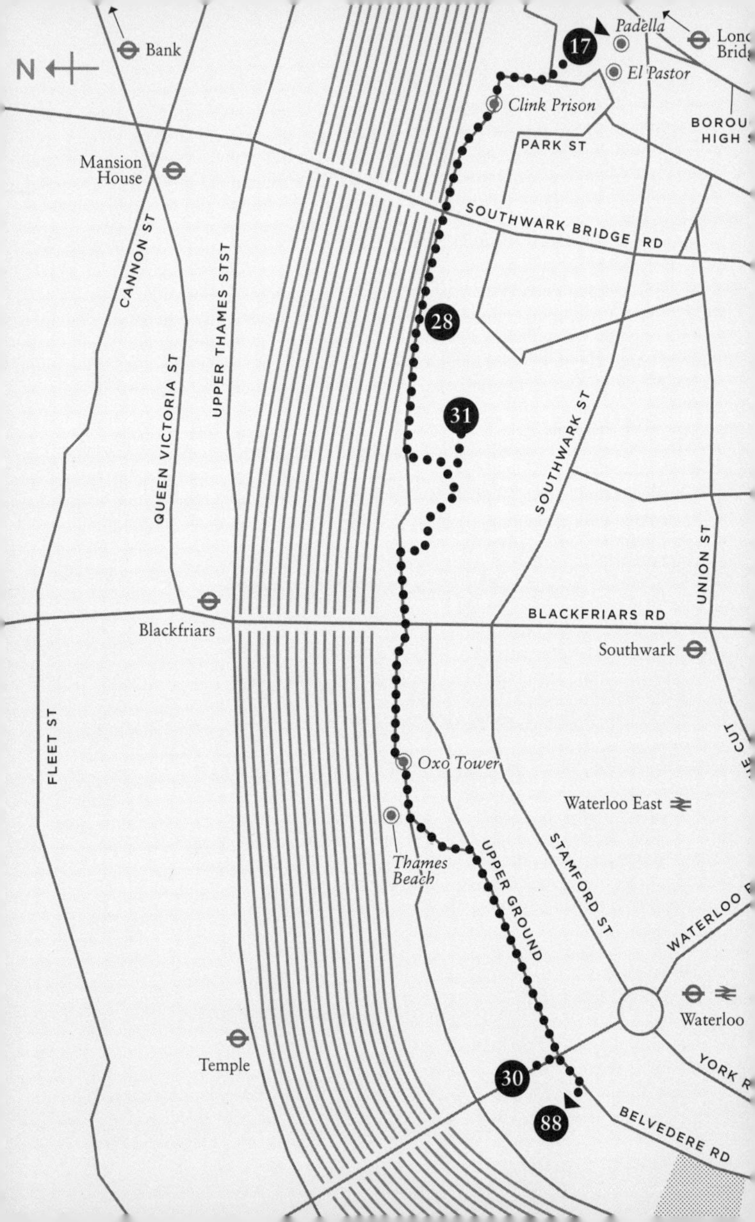

N
Bank
17
Padella
El Pastor
Clink Prison
PARK ST
Mansion House
SOUTHWARK BRIDGE RD
CANNON ST
UPPER THAMES STST
QUEEN VICTORIA ST
28
31
SOUTHWARK ST
UNION ST
Blackfriars
BLACKFRIARS RD
Southwark
FLEET ST
Oxo Tower
Waterloo East
Thames Beach
UPPER GROUND
STAMFORD ST
Waterloo
Temple
YORK
30
88
BELVEDERE RD

WALK 2

South Bank cultural stroll:
London Bridge to Hungerford Bridge

Line your stomach with lunch at Borough Market 17, be it a pile of pasta from *Padella** or tacos tostadas at *El Pastor**. Wend your way riverwards up Clink Street – home of the notorious *Clink Prison**, now a popular museum. Continue west along the river, passing Shakespeare's Globe 28 (drop in for a guided tour if the mood takes you). Next, it's time for a mooch around Tate Modern's 31 free permanent displays and current Turbine Hall commission (book ahead to guarantee entry to any temporary exhibitions that catch your eye). When your head is full of art, hit the river path again, ambling past the *OXO Tower** and mudlarks on the *Thames Beach**, towards the Southbank Centre 30. Here you can check out trailblazing exhibitions at the Hayward Gallery, watch in wonder at the outdoor skatepark or enjoy cocktails with a view in the Queen Elizabeth Hall roof garden. Or, if the weather's less than lovely, make a beeline for the cosy BFI bar 88 – followed by a film, if you have the time.

Walking time: 0.5 hours, 1.6 miles
Total time with stops: 5–6 hours
**Not in guidebook: more info online*

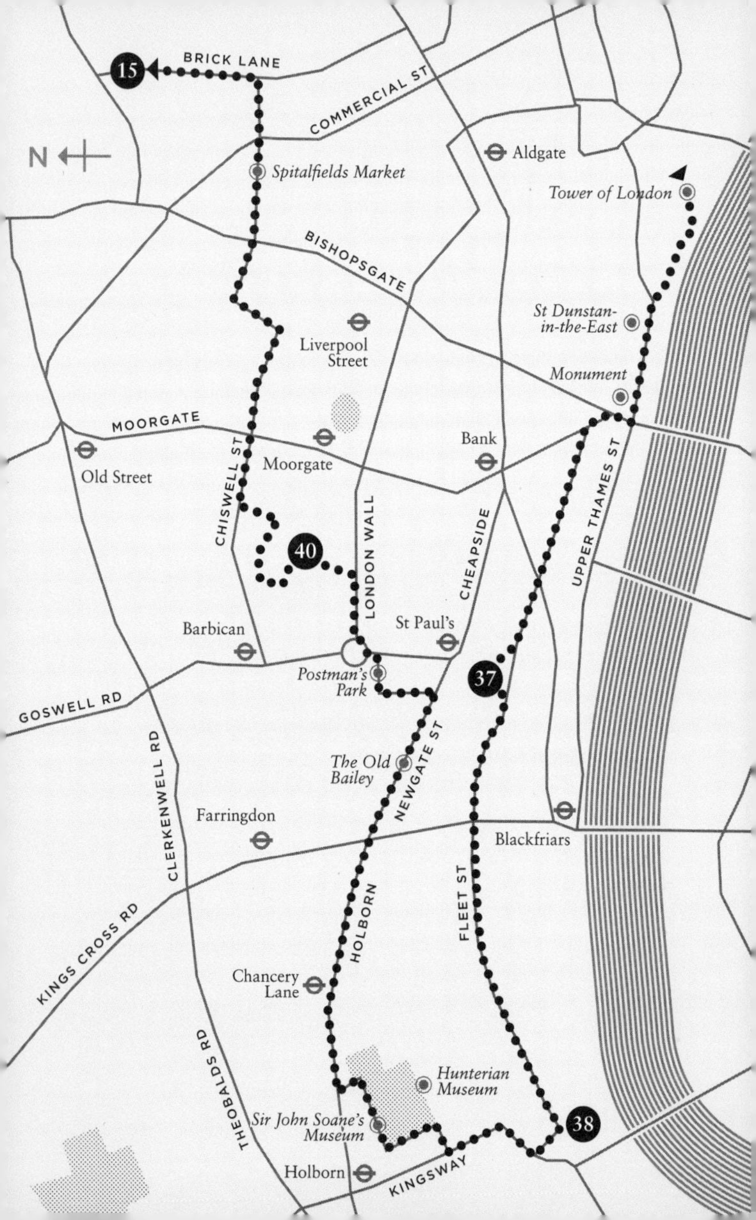
15
BRICK LANE
COMMERCIAL ST
N
Aldgate
Spitalfields Market
Tower of London
BISHOPSGATE
St Dunstan-
in-the-East
Liverpool
Street
Monument
MOORGATE
Bank
Old Street
Moorgate
CHISWELL ST
LONDON WALL
CHEAPSIDE
UPPER THAMES ST
40
Barbican
St Paul's
Postman's
Park
37
GOSWELL RD
The Old
Bailey
NEWGATE ST
CLERKENWELL RD
Farringdon
Blackfriars
FLEET ST
HOLBORN
KINGS CROSS RD
Chancery
Lane
THEOBALDS RD
Hunterian
Museum
Sir John Soane's
Museum
38
Holborn
KINGSWAY

WALK 3

Unearthing the City's rich history:
the Tower of London to Brick Lane

Where better to commence a historic tour of the capital than at the *Tower of London** – its oldest intact building, constructed between 1078 and 1399? Amble over to *St Dunstan's-in-the-East** – destroyed both by the Great Fire and the Blitz (and now a great place for a sandwich). On to *Monument** – the climbable tribute to those killed in the Great Fire of 1666, followed by a stroll around St Paul's Cathedral (37), built 1675–1710. Wander down Fleet Street to Somerset House (38), stopping for a coffee in the courtyard before heading inside to explore its latest exhibition. Continue towards Lincoln's Inn Fields, swinging by the brilliant (and free) *Sir John Soane's** or *Hunterian** museums and heading back east past the *Old Bailey** to *Postman's Park** – home to a profoundly moving Victorian memorial to heroic self-sacrifice. Next up, it's everyone's favourite Brutalist arts centre, the inimitable Barbican (40), for some architectural appreciation, followed by a stroll around *Spitalfields Market** and on to Brick Lane, concluding with a much-needed carb reload at the legendary Beigel Bake (15).

Walking time: 2 hours, 5.6 miles
Total time with stops: 6–8 hours
**Not in guidebook: more info online*

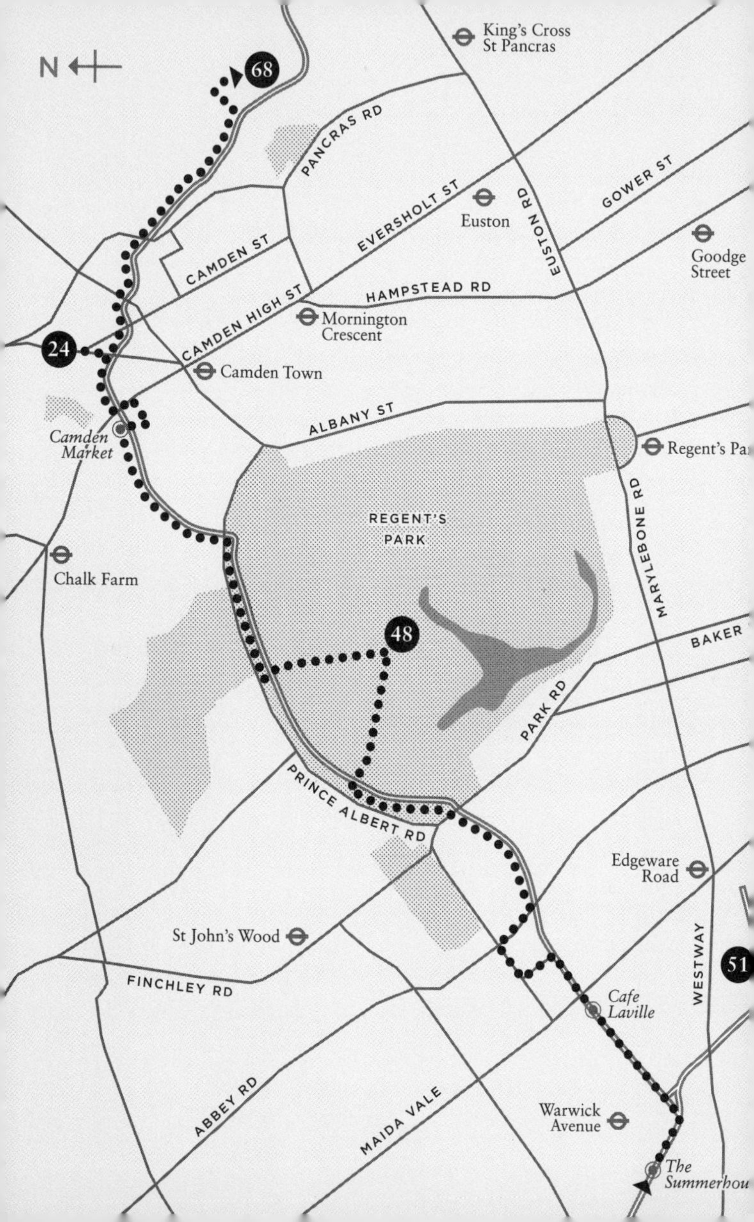

N
68
King's Cross St Pancras
PANCRAS RD
GOWER ST
EVERSHOLT ST
Euston
EUSTON RD
Goodge Street
CAMDEN ST
HAMPSTEAD RD
CAMDEN HIGH ST
Mornington Crescent
24
Camden Town
ALBANY ST
Camden Market
Regent's Pa
REGENT'S PARK
MARYLEBONE RD
Chalk Farm
48
BAKER
PARK RD
PRINCE ALBERT RD
Edgeware Road
St John's Wood
WESTWAY
51
FINCHLEY RD
Cafe Laville
ABBEY RD
MAIDA VALE
Warwick Avenue
The Summerhou

CYCLE 1

Cruise down the Regent's Canal: Little Venice to King's Cross

Begin your ride in Little Venice, where the Grand Union and Regent's canals converge. Load up on brunch classics at the *The Summerhouse** or sunny Italian dishes at *Cafe Laville** before swapping two wheels for a steering stick and embarking on a GoBoat 51 self-drive adventure. Hop back on your bike and coast along the Regent's Canal towpath to Regent's Park 48, where copious delights await. Head to the zoo in search of lions and ring-tailed lemurs, admire the many Regency terraces or simply flop on the grass with a book. Jump back in the saddle and proceed east via *Camden Market**, stopping to soak up the atmosphere and sample the diverse street food – Filipino ice cream spot Mamasons 24 is striking distance away if you fancy something sweet (and distinctly more serene). Once you've recovered from the hordes (or the sugar coma), pedal towards Coal Drops Yard 68, locking up your bike and settling in for an afternoon of shopping, snacking and summertime pints on the canal-side steps – or cutting-edge cocktails in one of the complex's bountiful bars.

Cycling time: 45 mins, 4.7 miles

Total time with stops: 2–4 hours

**Not in guidebook: more info online*

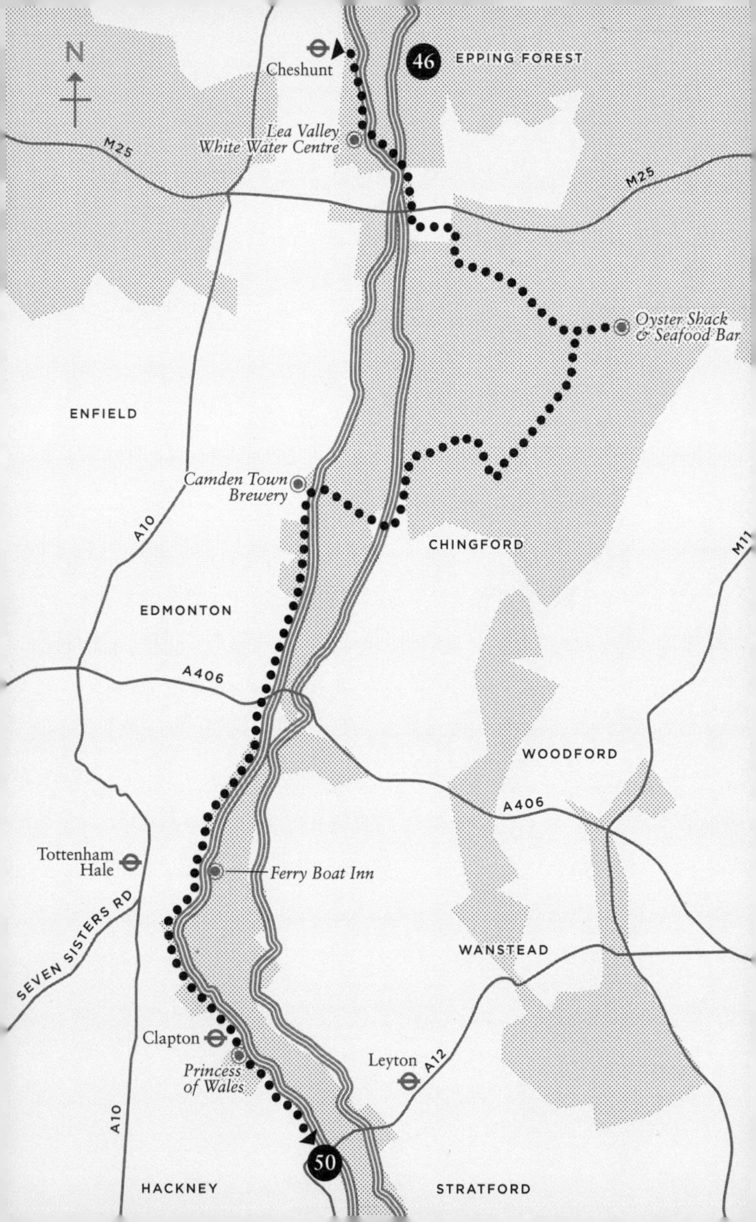
N
Cheshunt
46
EPPING FOREST
Lea Valley
White Water Centre
M25
M25
Oyster Shack
& Seafood Bar
ENFIELD
Camden Town
Brewery
A10
CHINGFORD
M11
EDMONTON
A406
WOODFORD
A406
Tottenham
Hale
Ferry Boat Inn
SEVEN SISTERS RD
WANSTEAD
Clapton
Princess
of Wales
Leyton
A12
A10
50
HACKNEY
STRATFORD

CYCLE 2

Following the River Lea: Epping Forest to Hackney Wick

Hop off the Overground at Cheshunt and straight onto your bike, heading south through Epping Forest (46) along the River Lee Navigation for three miles, past the *Lee Valley White Water Centre** (stop by for some kayaking if you're feeling bold) and eventually turning east towards High Beech. Drop by the *Oyster Shack & Seafood Bar** – a much-loved gem buried deep in the forest – for a box of juicy calamari, before jumping back on your bike and heading west through wildflower meadows until you hit the River Lea. Now pedal south, making time for a pint with a view at Enfield's sprawling *Camden Town Brewery**, Tottenham's *Ferry Boat Inn** or Clapton's buzzy *Princess of Wales**. Feeling refreshed? Continue cycling south through Clapton, past the Middlesex Filter Beds (ten points for spotting a Marsh Warbler) and Hackney Marshes, finally indulging in a well-earned evening sauna session at Hackney Wick's Community Sauna Baths (50) to soothe those tired muscles (check the website for special events spanning everything from storytelling to sound baths).

Cycling time: 2 hours, 18.5 miles

Total time with stops: 4–6 hours

**Not in guidebook: more info online*

1

ST. JOHN

Bold bastion of the city's foodie scene

The patron saint of loyalty is evidently looking down on his eponymous establishment – at least, that would be one explanation for St. JOHN's enduring success. Its three-decade reign as one of London's favourite restaurants might also be down to its sheer chutzpah. Founder Fergus Henderson is legendary for trailblazing nose-to-tail eating – a philosophy that sees chefs cheerfully plating up everything from trotters to pig hearts on the daily, not to mention its famed feast of bone marrow dolloped on hot toast. It's all served in a stripped-back dining room that does little to distract from the food. Order boldly (it's the only way to go), washing it all down with a glass of their plummy own-label claret and a bag of fresh madeleines to go.

26 St. John Street, ECIM 4AY
Nearest station: Farringdon
Other locations: Shoreditch, Marylebone
stjohnrestaurant.com

2

CHISHURU

Gobsmacking West African cuisine

'Chishuru' is a Hausa word that refers to the silence that falls when the food is too good to speak, which is exactly what you can expect from Adejoké 'Joké' Bakare's offbeat dishes. But while you may be rendered speechless with delight, Bakare's West African cooking is *noisy*, packed with fierce flavours and unexpected textures (she didn't become the first Black female chef to acquire a Michelin star by playing it safe). Order the set menu, which might include crisp àkàrà (bean) fritters stuffed with candied chillies and smashed morsels of plantain plunged in scotch bonnet sauce, and then chase it all down with a spiced okra martini – rationed to two per person lest they literally blow your head off.

3 Great Titchfield Street, W1W 8AX
Nearest station: Oxford Circus
chishuru.com

3

CADET

Mellow wine bar with picky bits

It might be a Cadet by name, but this laid-back spot is no rookie when it comes to wine. Opened in 2022 by celebrated natural wine importers Tom Beattie and Francis Roberts, ex St. JOHN chef Jamie Smart and master charcutier George Jephson, this neighbourhood bar is a favourite among Newington Greeners – but it's more than special enough to warrant a cross-city jaunt. Grab the gang and load up on classic pâté en croute, velvety mousse de canard on sourdough and anything that comes accompanied by Cadet's melty meringue wafers – all served up on charmingly mismatched crockery and washed down with something fresh and fruity (wines come by the glass, so you can sample the full spectrum). Bottoms up!

57 Newington Green, N16 9PX
Nearest station: Canonbury
cadetlondon.com

4

QUO VADIS

Iconic British dining

Literally translated from Latin, *quo vadis* means 'where are you going?', the answer to which should always be 'I'm going to Quo Vadis'. Established in 1926, this Soho stalwart oozes with history – its own and that of its building, which has housed both Karl Marx and a notorious brothel at various intervals. Helmed by feted chef Jeremy Lee since 2012, this atmospheric spot specialises in seasonal spins on classic British fare, with signatures including a generously stuffed smoked eel sandwich, decadent suet-crusted pie-of-the-day and an irresistibly nostalgic île flottante dessert, all served on charmingly monogrammed QV crockery (and, ideally, helped down with an Earl Grey martini). Vadis, ad nauseam.

26–29 Dean Street, W1D 3LL
Nearest station: Tottenham Court Road
quovadissoho.co.uk

HANS SLOANE
CHOCOLATEER

5

CAMBERWELL ARMS

Ultimate pub grub

A humdrum pub exterior does very little to deter the gannets from this elegant restaurant, where stylishly stripped-back interiors allow Chef Director Mike Davies' culinary masterpieces to do the talking. If they really did talk, Davies' dishes would probably be insufferable – such is the superiority of their ingredients, the polish of their presentation and their sheer deliciousness – but the pub's overarching vibe is one of humility, even despite its various accolades. Rouille-smothered mussels on toast, melt-in-the-mouth tempura pea pods and wickedly juicy pork crackling are just some of the unmissable pleasures on the seemingly mistitled 'Bar Snack' menu, while their two-person sharing roasts put the sun in Sunday lunch.

65 Camberwell Church Street, SE5 8TR
Nearest station: Denmark Hill
thecamberwellarms.co.uk

6

POPHAMS

Buns by day, bolognese by night

Baklava croissants and blood orange Danish. Hot apple crumbles and rosemary salt twists. This friendly neighbourhood bakery is responsible for more than a few of our favourite things – and unfortunately, we're not the only ones. In fact, it's not unusual to pop to Popham's mid-morning to find them sold out, with the early bird catching the maple-bacon swirl – Pophams' sweet 'n' salty best-seller. But man can't live by bread alone, and this branch is just as popular for its pasta as its pastry, with starchy smashes including a half-beetroot, half-gorgonzola doppio ravioli and a punchy plate of pistachio pesto-bound pea gnocchi. One to remember when you're feeling sad.

197 Richmond Road, E8 3NJ
Nearest station: London Fields
Other locations: Islington, Victoria Park
pophamsbakery.com

BOTTLE SHOP

7

E5 BAKEHOUSE

Ethical bread (and other good things)

Technically it's in E8, not E5, but that's the only thing that feels vaguely deceitful about this Hackney institution, housed in a trio of lofty railway arches beneath London Fields station. Indeed, transparency is key here and almost everything on sale is created from scratch, from the cakes and loaves made using flour stone-milled on site, to the coffee roasted at their Poplar sister site (staffed by participants of their refugee training programme) and daily-changing menu of wholesome dishes celebrating veg grown on their Suffolk farm. A lazy lunch in the walled back garden is always an afternoon well spent, and you categorically cannot leave without a loaf of that sourdough.

395–396 Mentmore Terrace, E8 3PH
Nearest station: London Fields
Other location: Poplar
e5bakehouse.com

HACK
WILD
STONE GROUND
MULTIGRAIN
A MIX OF FLOURS
+ SEEDS £4.20

8

THEO'S

Maximalist pizzas in minimalist surroundings

You'd be forgiven for strolling right past this Camberwell pizzeria with its whitewashed façade and simple signage. Thankfully there's nothing unremarkable about its pizzas, which come generously loaded and served in the form of crispy frittas (deep-fried pizzas), fat panuozzos (pizza sandwiches) and bubbly crusted classics. Menu regulars such as treacly aubergine and fiery nduja-topped pizzas are near-perfect, but it's the specials – crispy potatoes with lashings of pecorino fondue, creamed brussels sprouts encrusted with caciocavallo – where Theo's really rises to the occasion. Help it all down with a glass of orange wine and a big dollop of their legendary chilli sauce.

2 Grove Lane, SE5 8SY

Nearest station: Denmark Hill

Other location: Elephant & Castle

theospizzeria.com

9

MILDRED'S

The city's most vibrant vegan restaurant

It might be one of London's longest-surviving vegan restaurants, but Mildred's is young in spirit. Fully plant-based since 2021, this sustainably minded (but unsanctimonious) spot will satisfy even the staunchest of veggie sceptics with its fun, flavoursome and fulfilling dishes, which take their inspiration from every corner of the globe. Voyage to Mexico for finger-licking corn 'ribs' with hot mango sauce for dredging, to South Korea for tangy kimchi bokkeumbap (fried rice) and then to Tuscany for an authentic (and dairy-free) slice of tiramisu – or try the intercontinental tasting menu for a palate whistlestop tour. The place to take that friend who says they'll never go vegan.

9 Jamestown Road, NW1 7BW

Nearest station: Camden Town

Other locations: multiple, see website

mildreds.com

10

MORITO

Moreish Moorish tapas bar

There are tapas joints... and then there's Morito, Hackney Road's ever-popular Moorish bar and restaurant. Still reasonably priced in spite of its widespread acclaim, this is the sort of place where you'll want to order *everything*: tangy patatas bravas, chewy za'atar manakeesh (flat-bread), crispy chipirones (baby squid) and all. And while the food is dangerously good, there's so much more(ito) to this spot, from eclectic music nights in the downstairs dining room to a cocktail menu that will require serious self-restraint not to sample in its entirety. Head down on a sunny day for al fresco spritzes in the sun (not quite the Aegean, but close enough).

195 Hackney Road, E2 8JL
Nearest station: Hoxton
Other location: Exmouth Market
moritohackneyroad.co.uk

11

AKUB

Palestinian sharing plates

Notting Hill's pastel-hued terraces entice tourists and Instagrammers in their droves, but since 2023 there's been an even better reason to visit the colourful Uxbridge Street. Here, in appropriately olive green-fronted premises, Franco-Palestinian chef Fadi Kattan pays tribute to his homeland with a soul-nourishing dining experience filled with fragrance, flavour and fire. Fresh local produce and imported speciality ingredients combine to create modern twists on classic Palestinian dishes, from monkfish cured with arak (aniseed spirit) and bolstering spiced-squash dumplings to indulgent coffee-soaked toasted brioche piled with velvety laban and pistachios. Check the website for regular #CookForPalestine supper club events, whose proceeds support the humanitarian crisis in Gaza.

27 Uxbridge Street, W8 7TQ
Nearest station: Notting Hill Gate
akub-restaurant.com

12
SKETCH

Insta-famous dining rooms

Its toilets might be London's most TikTokked, but there's a lot more to Sketch than spending a penny in an egg pod (and then taking a selfie). Comprising two bars, two restaurants (one triple-Michelin-starred) and an afternoon tea lounge, all with their own idiosyncratic interiors, this photogenic favourite has something for every occasion. Proceed to the golden-hued Gallery for bottomless brews, petits gâteaux and inventive finger sandwiches; dine on succulent duck breast and champagne cocktails in the Glade's woodland wonderland; or go all out with hand-dived scallop carpaccio and Scottish langoustines, courtesy of the extravagant Lecture Room & Library's seven-course tasting menu. (But whatever you decide, be sure to excuse yourself for that all-important restroom shot.)

9 Conduit Street, W1S 2XG
Nearest station: Oxford Circus
sketch.london

13

SESSIONS ARTS CLUB

Enigmatic dining room, excellent food

Sessions is a fitting designation for a restaurant one could quite happily linger in all evening (and probably most of the next day). Set on the fourth floor of what was once the nation's largest courthouse, this former judge's dining room throbs with lightly faded grandeur – all peeling plasterwork, sweeping staircases and tastefully shabby armchairs. Despite the name, this isn't an exclusive members' club, but it *does* offer a delicious sense of privacy beginning at the inconspicuous entrance. Food is a communal feast of simple flavour fusions – blackcurrant-topped oysters, cognac-laced chocolate tart and duck pâté with a cherry on top. The actual cherry on top, however, is the picturesque summer terrace – the ideal spot for a melon martini.

4th Floor, 24 Clerkenwell Green, EC1R 0NA
Nearest station: Farringdon
sessionsartsclub.com

14

PAUL ROTHE & SON

Serious sandwich shop

This old-school Marylebone deli only deals in *proper*, *sensible* sandwiches. Family owned since 1900, the lunchbreak hotspot never fails to draw a crowd, despite its staunch refusal to bow to trends (and likely thanks to its very reasonable prices). Corned beef, prawn mayo and coronation chicken are just a few of the no-nonsense fillings the cheery staff insert between soft slices of homemade bread on the daily, but they'll gladly fill them with whatever weird and wonderful combination your belly desires – and upgrade you to ciabatta if you're feeling fancy. Come off-peak to peruse the deli shelves sans-crowds – and don't leave without a slice of their generously filled quiche.

35 Marylebone Lane, W1U 2NN
Nearest station: Bond Street
instagram.com/paulrotheandson

Cottage Delight
Speciality Foods

15

BEIGEL BAKE

24-hour bakery

The debate over which Brick Lane beigel shop reigns supreme will probably be raging until the end of days. If the weekend queues are anything to go by, 'the white one' just edges it over its (let's be honest, almost identical) yellow-fronted neighbour. Their salt beef signature is famous for a reason, its chewy casing bursting at the seams in its valiant efforts to support its contents: thickly sliced meat, tangy pickles and lashings of mayo and mustard. Don't neglect to sample Beigel Bake's other doughy offerings, be it the impossibly flaky apple turnover or the jaw-dislocating cheesecake. Head here at the end of a big night out... or for brunch the next morning.

159 Brick Lane, E1 6SB
Nearest station: Shoreditch High Street
bricklanebeigel.co.uk

HOT
BEIGELS
ALL NIGHT
BEIGEL BAKE
BRICK LANE BAKERY
No. 159
OPEN 24 HOURS 7 DAYS

TAKE AWAY
ONLY
HOT SALT BEEF

16

E. PELLICCI

Gilded greasy spoon

When only a full English will do, hotfoot it to this family-owned Italian caff. Friendly, loud and still drawing queues more than a century after Priamo Pellicci first flung open the doors, this Bethnal Green institution is as much an experience as it is an eatery, and counts Ray Winstone among its regulars. Now headed up by Priamo's grandchildren Nev and Anna, with their 'Mama' Maria head of the kitchen, the former Kray-brothers haunt still screams Old East End with its (now-listed) Art Deco interior and Vitrolite-panelled exterior, classic homecooked Britalian fare and staunch refusal to accept anything but cash. Order an 'Have the Lot' fry-up (in your best Cockney accent), followed by Mama's dessert of the day.

332 Bethnal Green Road, E2 0AG

Nearest station: Bethnal Green

epellicci.co.uk

E. PELLICCI

17

BOROUGH MARKET

Gastronomic wonderland

Gooey alfajores from Argentina. Baked cheeses from Bath. Conscious coffee from Colombia. This is one of the oldest and biggest food markets in London and undoubtedly its best. Travel the world with your tastebuds without so much as venturing beyond the shelter of the barrel-vaulted roof. A one-stop shop for gourmet ingredients, foodie gifts and adventurous lunches, this bustling 100-stall bazaar is always worth the elbow fight, whether you're lining up for a plate of Kappacasein's molten Raclette or awaiting one of Akara's fiery yet fluffy kuli kuli crab buns. Few things here are cheap, but generous free samples will ensure you select well – just be sure to bring an empty tote (and stomach).

8 Southwark Street, SE1 1TL
Nearest station: London Bridge
boroughmarket.org.uk

BRINDISA
BRINDISA
THE GINGER
SAUSAGE

18

THE DRAPERS ARMS

Serious food and wine in chic surrounds

That Grayson Perry is a regular might be all you need to know about this appropriately elegant neighbourhood pub, whose dollhouse-like façade implores popping in, whether you'd intended to or not. But the elegant aesthetic belies a meaty core, its stripped-back decor standing in stark contrast with its decidedly maximalist wine menu and substantial plates of food. Plump (probably quite literally) for whatever suet-crusted pie is on that day, chased by a dark, dense slice of chocolate stout cake and a glass of silky pinot noir. Because, if you're going to *pub*, you might as well do it properly.

44 Barnsbury Street, N1 1ER
Nearest station: Caledonian Road & Barnsbury
thedrapersarms.com

Freehouse
THE DRAPERS ARMS
Dining Room

19

ROCHELLE CANTEEN

Feasting in a former school bike shed

Inside a converted bike shed, within a former school, across a little green, behind an unassuming gate, at the heart of the world's first social housing estate (ring the bell for entry), you'll discover a restaurant you simply cannot miss. Lesser establishments would struggle in such a clandestine setting, but Rochelle's fresh, fun, fuss-free food is as popular today as it was two decades ago, with reservations snapped up well ahead of time. Should you succeed in securing a table (and locating it), order voraciously from the daily-changing menu, whose revered regulars include seared sardines sweetened with blood orange and silky, charred aubergine enveloped in unctuous labneh. Perhaps we should have kept this one to ourselves...

16 Playground Gardens, E2 7FA
Nearest station: Shoreditch High Street
rochellecanteen.com

BOYS
ROCHELLE
CANTEEN
OPEN FOR
BREAKFAST
&
LUNCH

20

MARKSMAN

Gastropub that's on the money

Standard pub grub not hitting the spot? Aim higher at the Marksman, a juiced-up Hackney boozer helmed by acclaimed St. JOHN alumni Tom Harris and Jon Rotheram, who bagged London's first ever Michelin Pub of the Year award just months after taking the reins. And if you think that's impressive, prepare to have your taste-buds blown by its face-sized Yorkshire puddings, almost conceitedly crisp fried potatoes and banging beef and barley buns, all savoured in the stylish surrounds of the first-floor dining room. Or simply pop into the wood-panelled downstairs pub for an impromptu pint… or a bottle of barrel-aged beaujolais.

254 Hackney Road, E2 7SJ
Nearest station: Hoxton
marksmanpublichouse.com

Marksman

21

POCKETS

Perfect pitas

Think standing in line for 30 minutes in pursuit of pita is madness? What if that pita is so preposterously puffy it could double as a pillow and comes so overstuffed you ponder, as you grasp it with both hands, how best to get it in your mouth – and not down your front? What if the fillings, a far cry from your standard kebab shop fare, comprise nutty rounds of freshly fried falafel, an almost offensively large, hot, blackened chilli and a surprising but satisfying disc of deep-fried potato, all generously drizzled with creamy tahini and tangy mango pickle the colour of a Sicilian sunset? Missing out on all that – now *that* would be madness.

367 Mentmore Terrace, E8 3RT

Nearest station: London Fields

instagram.com/pockets_uk

22

JOLENE

Your pastry is beyond compare

It's almost impossible to visit an outpost of this beloved neighbourhood bakery without humming Dolly Parton's heartbreaker under your breath. It's even harder to leave without a pastry, whether it's a perfectly pillowy cream bun or a death row-worthy Danish. And really, why leave when you could stick around for a plate of fat sardines scooped up with fluffy focaccia and washed down with a satisfyingly sour glass of vermillion wine, or a pistachio-bejewelled pork terrine liberally loaded onto crusty baguette? Daily menu changes make regular trips unavoidable – and before you know it, you'll be talking about it in your sleep.

324 Hornsey Road, N7 7HE
Nearest station: Finsbury Park
Other location: Newington Green
bigjobakery.com

23

TOAD BAKERY

Dough of your dreams

You've got to eat a lot of substandard pastries before you find your devastatingly handsome cornbread croissant and ride off into the sunset (or at least hop on the 345) together. Beginning life in 2021 as a pop-up named Frog, TOAD has all the components of a fairy-tale bakery: delightful staff, heavenly sourdough, robust coffee and an ever-changing assortment of freshly baked and wildly inventive sweet and savoury treats, from Boursin escargot pastries to giant Jaffa cakes. On the downside, everyone in Camberwell (and beyond) wants a slice of the action, so use your loaf and get here before the queues form.

44 Peckham Road, SE5 8PX
Nearest station: Denmark Hill
toadbakery.com

24

MAMASONS

Filipino ice cream parlour

The words 'dirty ice cream' lit up in pink and blue neon may be off-putting to some but, rest assured, it's nothing to do with this cult parlour's hygiene standards. Keeping Kentish Town sweet since 2017, the now-expanded Filipino favourite deals in sorbetes: hand-churned coconut-milk (or in the Philippines, carabao milk) ice-cream, nicknamed 'dirty' because it's traditionally made at home and sold on the streets. The ube (purple yam) sorbetes ice-cream sandwich is popular for a reason, but the Halo Halo (a sort of exotic trifle in a cup) is just as decadent. Or simply grab a vat of your favourite flavour – including black buko (coconut blended with charcoal) or salty, creamy queso – to devour straight from the tub. *Pure filth.*

91 Kentish Town Road, NW1 8NY
Nearest station: Camden Road, Camden Town
Other locations: Shepherd's Bush, Chinatown
dirtyicecream.co.uk

MAMASONS

25

BAO

Idiosyncratic Taiwanese cafe

Wes Anderson vibes abound at this iconic steamed bun spot, whose delightful mid-century interiors would eclipse a lesser restaurant's cuisine. But just as the filmmaker's output offers style *and* substance, BAO's moreish morsels are somehow even more palatable than their surrounds – and, if anything, even prettier. Triumphs include a surprisingly spicy Taiwanese chicken Kiev, a satisfyingly sweet plate of maple-smeared fries and BAO's signature sad-face custard bun – star of many an Instagram feed. And let's not forget the main event: delicious mounds of perfectly seasoned pork, fish, beef, prawn or daikon, bookended by warm, fluffy bao (much like a burger, but better). Look out for the impossibly cute limited-edition buns.

4 Pancras Square, N1C 4DP
Nearest station: King's Cross St. Pancras
Other locations: multiple, see website
baolondon.com

26

KOYA

Unpretentious Japanese canteen

A queue snakes out the door of this cosy Soho noodle spot every lunchtime – and that's probably all the impetus you need to join the back of it. The udon (Koya's speciality) is chunky, chewy and delicious served cold with a creamy sesame dip or steaming hot in a comforting broth topped with juicy prawn tempura. The noodles pair splendidly with tangy small plates such as the ume-boshi (salted plums) and Kakuni (cider-braised pork). Bar-side seating and a buzzy but relaxed vibe make this an ideal spot for a quiet solo lunch or a casual date – just try not to dribble too much down your chin if it's the latter.

50 Frith Street, W1D 4SQ

Nearest station: Tottenham Court Road

Other locations: London Fields, Bank

koya.co.uk

27

LYLE'S

Exquisite set menu meals

You gotta have faith, as George Michael insisted. He probably wasn't talking about this zeitgeisty restaurant in Shoreditch, but a little bit of faith in an outwardly rather sparse establishment that charges usurious prices for food you don't get to pick yourself seems wise. As luck (and a Michelin star) would have it, Lyle's is well worthy of that trust – and the price tag. Its set menu is surprising – salty rock oysters stuffed with tangy crab apple granita, a gleaming pheasant broth bejewelled with a buttery egg yolk and a pile of jammy figs crowned with a scoop of self-referential fig ice cream – but it's reliably, drool-inducingly good. And if none of that can convince you, try a minimum-commitment, maximum-impact à la carte lunch instead.

Tea Building, 56 Shoreditch High Street, E1 6JJ
Nearest station: Shoreditch High Street
lyleslondon.com

28

SHAKESPEARE'S GLOBE

Open-air playhouse

All the world's a stage, but when it comes to the works of Shakespeare there's only one place to experience them. Built just moments from the original Globe, this faithful reconstruction has staged dazzling productions of every one of the Bard's plays over its 27-year run, from traditional adaptations to modern reinventions and everything in between. Famed for its audience participation, the timber-framed, thatch-roofed amphitheatre offers the ultimate immersive experience, with family-friendly performances and tickets for as little as £5 for those who are happy to stand. The only question is what to see – or not to see.

21 New Globe Walk, SE1 9DT
Nearest station: London Bridge
shakespearesglobe.com

29

BRITISH MUSEUM

Bloomsbury bastion of human history

Contrary to its name, you'll find artefacts hailing from virtually every country on the planet at this sprawling museum, with many of them acquired during the expansion of the British Empire. But despite such controversial origins (and an on-going debate around repatriating objects), the museum's hoard never fails to pull in the hordes, making for an overwhelming – and often infuriating – outing if you're underprepared. Get ahead of the crowd and plan before you go, being sure to add the charismatic Lewis chessmen, mesmerising Egyptian mummies and cryptic Rosetta Stone – the tablet that unlocked the secret of Egyptian hieroglyphs – to your itinerary.

Great Russell Street, WC1B 3DG
Nearest stations: Holborn, Russell Square
britishmuseum.org

30

SOUTHBANK CENTRE & HAYWARD GALLERY

Brutalist beacon of liberal arts

Galvanising gigs! Dynamic dance performances! Provocative poetry readings! Affecting art exhibitions! This vibrant arts centre has it all, with events that will make you feel *alive*, whatever your cultural appetite. Refreshingly inclusive, its programme regularly spotlights the work of LGBTQ+, Black, disabled and other minority-group artists, making it the ideal place to shirk the status quo. For families, February's Imagine Children's Festival and the summertime fountain maze are obligatory, while the Hayward's fantastical exhibitions (past offerings have included a futurist Lee Bul dreamscape and a Carsten Höller-constructed playground) deliver the ultimate escapism.

Belvedere Road, SE1 8XX
Nearest station: Waterloo
southbankcentre.co.uk

HAYWARD GALLERY
Gursky

31
TATE MODERN

Electrifying art in former power station

Partial to Picasso? Devoted to Dalí? Bow down to your art idols at this vast cathedral of creativity, whose free-to-enter permanent collection delivers an electrifying crash course in contemporary art. Beyond the basics, Tate's reliably impressive paid exhibitions are well worth the membership fee, with recent hits including a deep dive into the world of environmental artist Olafur Eliasson and the largest Yoko Ono retrospective ever shown in the UK. And you can't possibly miss the Turbine Hall, the gallery's cavernous core, whose annual artist commissions have seen it commandeered by everything from 30-foot spiders to alien jellyfish drones. *God bless modern art.*

Bankside, SE1 9TG
Nearest station: Blackfriars
tate.org.uk

32

VICTORIA & ALBERT MUSEUM

5,000 years of art and design

It's been welcoming visitors since its royal namesakes were alive and kicking – with many of its objects dating back to antiquity – and yet this iconic institution feels anything but fusty. No one does blockbuster exhibitions quite like the Victoria & Albert Museum, with iconic erstwhile shows including a moving Alexander McQueen retrospective and a spellbinding survey of Tim Walker's fashion photography. Even its permanent displays feel fresh, be it the dazzling jewellery collection or the recently revamped Raphael Court, home to the Master's beguiling cartoons. Once your cultural appetite is sated, fill your belly in the opulent Gamble Room – the world's first ever museum–cafe (and the best place to scoff a scone).

Cromwell Road, SW7 2RL

Nearest station: South Kensington

vam.ac.uk

33
HAMPTON COURT PALACE

Myths, mazes and monarchs

You'd think the favourite home of English history's most mesmerising monarch would be a decent bet for a fun day out – and you'd be right! Henry VIII's beloved palace pulsates with character. The site of numerous marriages and divorces (all Henry's), plus other momentous historical events, it's easy to bring the past to life, whether you're picturing royal banquets in the hammer-beamed Great Hall or trying to catch sight of Catherine Howard's ghost in the eerie Haunted Gallery. Beyond the palace walls, the enigmatic hedge maze summons escapism, 18th-century style, while the myths-and-legends-themed playground invites kids to defeat dragons, commandeer lofty towers and generally live like kings.

Hampton Court Way, East Molesey, KT8 9AU
Nearest station: Hampton Court
hrp.org.uk

34

WHITECHAPEL GALLERY

Cutting-edge contemporary art

The chaos of Whitechapel Road belies the tranquillity of this ever-surprising gallery. It initiated the careers of 'living sculptures' Gilbert and George more than 50 years ago, among countless other prodigies during its near 125-year reign. Constant innovation is a fundamental consideration of this vibrant space, which shuns a permanent collection over a dynamic programme of temporary exhibitions (recent highlights have included Theaster Gates' multimedia homage to clay and Elmgreen & Dragset's abandoned swimming pool). The gallery bookshop keeps things just as fresh, while in-house restaurant Townsend follows suit with a daily-changing menu of seasonal delights.

77–82 Whitechapel High Street, E1 7QX
Nearest station: Aldgate East
whitechapelgallery.org

THE PASSMORE EDWARDS
LIBRARY
UNDERGROUND
ALDGATE EAST STATION
Whitechapel Gallery

35

SOUTH LONDON GALLERY

Pioneering exhibition space

Its eponymy says a lot about this spectacular art gallery, which dazzles with its international programme while radiating a distinctly Peckham air of cool. Dedicated to contemporary work since the 1990s, SLG has hosted many significant art moments in the last couple of decades, from Tracey Emin's infamous *Everyone I Have Ever Slept With* to Thomas Hirschhorn's post-apocalyptic *In-Between*. Kick off your art journey at the light-filled Fire Station space before heading to the architecturally distinct (yet no less impressive) main gallery building, finishing with melt-in-the-mouth pastries at South London Louie – brunch favourite Louie Louie's stylish SLG outpost.

65–67 Peckham Road, SE5 8UH
Nearest station: Peckham Rye
southlondongallery.org

WELCOME TO THE SLG

36
NATIONAL PORTRAIT GALLERY

Britain in more than 1,000 faces

Social rights activists, feminist icons, silver-screen legends and Tudor monarchs assemble on the walls of this captivating gallery – the home of the most comprehensive portrait collection on the planet. Fresh-faced following a three-year revamp, the re-energised NPG is more accessible, diverse and altogether more representative of the UK today, with an entire gallery dedicated to female sitters. Head straight for the History Makers Now display – a powerful who's who of contemporary changemakers – before embarking on a free tour of the gallery's most illustrious occupants, from Anne Boleyn to the Brontës.

St. Martin's Place, WC2H OHE
Nearest station: Charing Cross
npg.org.uk

THE JULIA AND HANS RAUSING GALLERY

37

ST. PAUL'S CATHEDRAL

Domed masterpiece

While faith in God is not a prerequisite for visiting this legendary landmark, a willingness to suspend your disbelief for the duration probably should be. Indeed, whatever your convictions, it's hard to accept that you have not in fact ascended to heaven upon entering the cathedral's (admittedly not very pearly) gates. And while you could simply take a pew and absorb the potent sense of peace, there are many more virtuous pastimes to relish here, from beholding spiritually inspired artworks to confessing secrets in the Whispering Gallery or heeding a choir of veritable angels at one of the cathedral's free daily Evensong services. A positively divine day out, however you choose to spend it.

St. Paul's Churchyard, EC4M 8AD
Nearest station: St. Paul's
stpauls.co.uk

38

SOMERSET HOUSE

Grand Georgian arts destination

There's nowhere in town like Somerset House. In fact, there's nowhere in the world like it. That is, unless you count the Georgian quadrangle, which could plausibly double as a Roman piazza in the summer months when the cafe spills outside and children gambol in the sprawling fountains, or as a Viennese square come winter, when the water jets give way to a spellbinding ice rink and fairy-tale Christmas tree. Then there's the enduringly otherworldly exhibition programme, which has deftly transported visitors everywhere from Beanotown to the Peanuts universe – and even to Hell, courtesy of its wonderfully warped *Horror Show*. In between, pop down for absorbing talks, performances and innumerable other ways to dodge reality.

Strand, WC2R 1LA
Nearest station: Temple
somersethouse.org.uk

39

DESIGN MUSEUM

A century of creative ingenuity

Rubik's cube. Beck's map of the tube. Rietveld's chair. Barbie's hair. If it's a design classic, you'll find it at this vast archive of problem-solving creativity. Take a whistlestop tour through the last 100 years of design, courtesy of the museum's illuminating permanent displays, or sink your teeth into one of its meaty temporary exhibitions, whose recent highlights have included a deep dive into Kubrick's cinematography, a study of the enduring popularity of sneakers and even a speculative look at a move to Mars. No doubt you'll have designs on the contents of the brilliant museum store, but the occasional pop-up shops, which have included a Camille Walala-designed supermarket and a Barbie doll boutique, demand a dedicated daytrip.

224–238 Kensington High Street, W8 6AG
Nearest station: High Street Kensington
designmuseum.org

DESIGNER

40

BARBICAN CENTRE

Concrete colossus of culture

Brutalism buffs will be happy enough pounding its high-rise pedways, admiring its architectural angles and caressing its coarse façade, but there's plenty to recommend the Barbican beyond its iconic concrete shell. Take, for instance, its gloriously green conservatory, a vast indoor rainforest whose verdant walkways are what Sunday (and Friday) strolls were made for. Or its cutting-edge galleries, whose recent exhibits have explored subjects as diverse as the politics of textiles and the climate emergency. And then there's the equally varied programme of live performance, which spans immersive baby theatre through to orchestral drum and bass. Still thinking about that concrete shell? Join an enlightening architectural tour for a peek behind the veneer.

Silk Street, EC2Y 8DS
Nearest station: Barbican
barbican.org.uk

41

HAMPSTEAD HEATH

North London's wild wonder

Stately homes. Swimming. Sham bridges. Skylines. So plentiful are the delights of this magnificently untamed park, you could roam its 800 acres every day of your life and never grow tired (at least, not cerebrally). The Heath's often-treacherous terrain can prove physically exhausting, but its rewards are well worth the schlep: panoramic views atop Parliament Hill, illustrious artworks at Kenwood House, the major endorphin rush that follows an outdoor dip in the magical ponds or modernist lido. Head down on Saturdays for fresh blooms and lavender macarons from the bustling farmers' market, or flee the crowds in pursuit of faded grandeur at the century-old Hill Garden and Pergola.

Nearest stations: Hampstead Heath, Gospel Oak

cityoflondon.gov.uk

42

GREENWICH PARK

Culture-rich green space

History comes vividly to life in Greenwich Park, a former Tudor hunting ground that's home to not one, but *three* royal museums. Part of the Maritime Greenwich World Heritage site and the oldest of London's eight Royal Parks, this breathtaking beauty spot affords visitors the chance to lock eyes with Tudor monarchs, courtesy of the Queen's House's sizeable art collection; straddle time zones at the Royal Observatory; behold Nelson's bullet-punctured jacket at the National Maritime Museum; and even blast off to outer space at the state-of-the-art planetarium. The park's calf-crushingly steep Point Hill is also a strong contender for the best views of the London skyline... just don't tell Hampstead Heath (no.41).

Nearest stations: Maze Hill, Cutty Sark

royalparks.org.uk

43

VICTORIA PARK

Food, festivals and fountain frolics

Though built to serve working class East Enders, this much-loved green space is far from a local secret 180 years on. Host to annual music festivals such as Field Day and All Points East, the aptly dubbed 'People's Park' draws revellers from every corner of the capital in the summer months, when rowboats and pedalos scatter its vast lake and children romp in its swirling concrete play fountain. Out of season, warm your cockles with one of foodie favourite Pavilion's fiery Sri Lankan brunches, or install yourself in one of three cosy pubs that line the park's 2.7-mile periphery (the People's Park Tavern has princely roasts and a roaring log fire).

Nearest stations: Mile End,
Bethnal Green, Hackney Wick
towerhamlets.gov.uk

44

KEW GARDENS

Horticultural heaven

It might boast more botanical specimens than any garden on the planet, but a passion for plants isn't a precondition for a fruitful visit to Kew. Anyone with an appetite for dramatic Victorian architecture, cutting-edge art, inventive children's play spaces or just some peace and quiet will be well served by the 330-acre garden, which counts a vertigo-inducing treetop walkway, indoor rainforest and immersive 'beehive' (a 56-foot-tall installation in a wildflower meadow) among its star attractions. Supposing you do have a fervour for flora, don't leave without sniffing out Kew's sweet-smelling woodland bluebells (spring) and Rose Garden (summer), or its seriously stinky 'corpse flower' (in bloom for just 36 hours every 1-2 years). Either way, it's a lush day out.

Nearest station: Kew Gardens

kew.org

45

PRIMROSE HILL

Superb park with sublime summit

Blur lauded its 'nice' views. Sylvia Plath eulogised its golden leaves. William Blake claimed to have 'conversed with the spiritual sun' here (his words are now carved in stone at the hill's apex). It's not hard to see why Primrose Hill inspires poetry. Ascending its grassy mound, mortal worries seem to evaporate as fast as the city grows Lilliputian in the distance. And while the park is arguably best enjoyed in the summer months, over a picnic procured from one of Regent's Park Road's many independent delis, it's just as breathtaking come November, when its protected views allow for some serious (and totally free) firework gazing.

Nearest stations: Camden Town,
Swiss Cottage, St. John's Wood
royalparks.org.uk

46

EPPING FOREST

Sprawling ancient woodland

Pondering which of this bewitching site's 6,000 acres to explore first? Give up the guesswork with one of its ten circular waymarked trails, be it a soothing stroll from picturesque High Beach rounded off with a cold pint and juicy platter from hidden treasure the Oyster Shack & Seafood Bar, a tot-friendly ramble across open grassland or a more challenging 6-mile trek via the forest's enchanting deer sanctuary. More invested in history than hiking? Soak up some Tudor charm at Queen Elizabeth's Hunting Lodge (followed by a brunch fit for a queen at the adjacent barn cafe) or follow in the fearless footsteps of Boudicca at one of the site's duo of atmospheric Iron Age settlements.

Nearest stations: Epping,
Chingford, Theydon Bois
visiteppingforest.org

47

BATTERSEA PARK

The whole nine (hundred thousand) yards

Yes, it's home to one of the capital's largest playgrounds – but you could argue that this buzzy riverside park is just one *giant* playground, so plentiful are its amusements. Besides the epic children's area, which will thrill both tots and teens, the 200-acre (or 968,000-yard) oasis boasts a much-loved children's zoo, an exhilarating tree-top challenge and chances to speed through the park on a Segway or feel the rush of a recumbent ride. Prefer a leisurelier pace? Try a stroll around the iconic Buddhist Peace Pergola. Or grab one of the Pear Tree cafe's lake-side tables and watch the pedalos pass with a fat pile of pancakes.

SW11 4NJ

Nearest stations: Battersea Park, Queenstown Road

batterseapark.org

48

REGENT'S PARK

Pleasure and peace in princely surrounds

Much like its namesake, the notoriously extravagant Prince Regent (King George IV), this lavishly landscaped, villa-lined oasis is famed for its visual opulence and plentiful cultural pastimes. It's a darned sight more popular than the prince, and you'll find its charismatic zoo, quirky playgrounds and outdoor theatre (Britain's oldest) reliably packed. However, just like George, the park has its fair share of secrets. Find your zen on the atmospheric (and typically deserted) Japanese island or procure some privacy in the delightfully date-worthy grounds of the neoclassical St. John's Lodge. And if the annual Frieze fair feels a bit too frantic, get your art fix at the outdoor Frieze Sculpture show, its infinitely calmer, more down-to-earth sibling.

Nearest stations: Regent's Park, Baker Street

royalparks.org.uk

49

HYDE PARK

Urban utopia

Central London has its charms, but it would be utterly insufferable without its sprawling back garden. At various times a Tudor hunting ground, Great Exhibition venue and the site of countless gory public hangings at the Tyburn Gallows, heavenly Hyde Park is these days characterised by its capacity for total, blissful freedom. Wild about wild swimming? Take the plunge at the Serpentine Lido. Massive melomaniac? Dance on down to the annual British Summer Time festival. Passionate about... literally anything at all? Make like Marx and Orwell and voice your views at the world-famous Speakers' Corner. Or just delve into all the glorious greenery.

Nearest stations: Hyde Park Corner,
Lancaster Gate, Marble Arch
royalparks.org.uk

50

COMMUNITY SAUNA BATHS

Let off some steam

When your body needs TLC, but you don't want to spend an arm and a leg, book yourself into this friendly outdoor spa. Set up to bring the innumerable benefits of Finnish sauna culture to the masses, this inclusive complex is open for affordable contrast bathing come rain or shine, with six rustic saunas and a selection of ice-cold plunge pools to really get your blood pumping. Regular storytelling, sound baths, and trans and queer events mean there's something for everyone, with a keen emphasis on community (the clue is in the name). But don't sweat it if you're feeling less than sociable: the silent sauna, optional one-on-one treatments and adjoining coworking cafe are all perfect for lone bathers.

80 Eastway, E9 5JH
Nearest station: Hackney Wick
Other locations: Stratford, Bermondsey, Peckham
community-sauna.co.uk

Treehouse
Be mindful
of others
experience

51

GOBOAT

Self-drive boat rental

Thames tours are a tourist requisite, but nothing beats skippering your own motorboat around north London's leafy canals. Requiring zero prior seafaring experience, these fully electric pleasure boats set sail from Paddington Basin, with two-hour hires allowing for a relatively leisurely cruise north-east to Camden Lock via the ever-so-creepy Maida Hill Tunnel, past the monkey valley that marks the start of London Zoo and the mansions that line Regent's Park, and back again. Captain hats are included – all you need is a picnic and a gang of (up to seven) mates.

Merchant Square, W2 1AS
Nearest station: Paddington
Other locations: multiple, see website
goboat.co.uk

TORELLI

52

THE CASTLE CLIMBING CENTRE

Majestic climbing, both indoors and out

London isn't short of climbing walls, but how many can say they inhabit a real-life castle? Ok, so technically this Hackney landmark was built to filter sewage, per the Victorians' penchant for making their pumping stations look like palaces, but its imposing architecture certainly makes for a majestic climbing experience. Unswervingly popular, the Castle has been hosting top-rope and lead-climbing fanatics for nearly three decades and boasts a dizzying 450 routes alongside an exhilarating bouldering offer that extends into its capacious garden. Come for the workout, the giddy heights and the chance to climb in the sun; stay for the buzzy events programme and wholesome post-climb rewards from the on-site veggie cafe.

Green Lanes, N4 2HA
Nearest station: Manor House
castle-climbing.co.uk

22

53

ARTWORDS

Independent arts bookshop

You shouldn't judge a book by its cover but it's hard not to at this vibey bookshop, whose colour-coordinated book-cover window displays are often the very thing that lures you in. Engrossing London Fields' creative citizens since 2001, Artwords is, true to its name, concerned largely with the visual arts and culture. Stock spans everything from coffee-table photography compendiums to edifying essay collections, cult zines and beautifully illustrated children's books – mostly from independent publishers. Bookmark their Instagram page for the first word on colourful new releases and buzzy launch events.

20–22 Broadway Market, E8 4QJ

Nearest station: London Fields

Other location: Hackney Central

artwords.co.uk

MAP STORIES
QUEER
illuminature
PUNK LONDON 1977.
BROOKS
François

54

CHOOSING KEEPING

Sophisticated stationery

The Digital Age has its benefits, but there are still few things more satisfying than selecting new stationery, be it an unblemished notebook or a box-fresh pencil case. Beginning life as a tiny boutique on Columbia Road, this since-relocated (and significantly expanded) store heaves with back-to-school nostalgia. Cheese-shaped erasers from Czechia, precision scissors from Japan, hand wood-blocked decorative papers from Paris and artisanal paperweights from NYC are just a handful of the analogue delights you're unlikely to find elsewhere, making choosing practically impossible. *Keeping* your purchases for years to come, though – that's a given.

21 Tower Street, WC2H 9NS
Nearest station: Leicester Square
choosingkeeping.com

55

PRESENT & CORRECT

Think outside the (pencil) box

Like the adult version of a sweet shop, this enticing stationery boutique threatens to pilfer all your pocket money. A Holborn fixture since 2012, Present & Correct is a papyrophiliac's paradise, with rare vintage collectables, contemporary office accessories and quirky finds from across the globe all delightfully arranged as though they were office-supply pick 'n' mix. A favourite among design-conscious students and houseproud WFH-ers, this stylish store is as much of a destination for gift-seekers, with whale-shaped Italian staplers, 60-year-old Bulgarian folk stamps and Dutch-designed minimalist planners among its sweetest treats.

12 Bury Place, WC1A 2JL
Nearest station: Holborn
presentandcorrect.com

1–365
Things To Do Today
Day Plan

56

LIBERTY

Luxury department store

Florals may not be ground-breaking, but there's a lot more to Liberty than its flowery fabrics. Open since 1875, this eccentric emporium presents a shopping experience like no other – one that's more akin to ransacking a treasure-laden merchant ship or visiting a well-travelled aunt's country pile and rifling through her amassed souvenirs. An idle browse around its six fascinating floors is uplifting whatever the season, but it's in September, when the beloved Christmas chintz shop opens its doors, that it's at its most magical. Prices aren't for the faint of heart (or light of pocket) but it's always well worth the investment, whether you're grabbing a posh tin of biscuits or splashing out on some serious bling.

Regent Street, W1B 5AH
Nearest station: Oxford Circus
libertylondon.com

LIBERTY
LIBERTY
LIBERTY

57

DAUNT BOOKS

Awe-inspiring bookstore

Its three galleried levels of towering tomes and curious insistence on arranging titles by country – rather than alphabetically – can mean this iconic branch of London's beloved indie bookstore tends to live up to its name. But look beyond its intimidating interior (its decor survives from what's thought to be the world's first custom-built bookshop) and its 'novel' way of doing things, and Daunt will soon be in your good books. The former travel bookstore still stocks a mind-boggling array of wanderlust-prompting titles, but whatever your genre you'll find it here – just be prepared to bag more than you bargained for (speaking of which, a Daunt tote is a Londoner's staple).

83–84 Marylebone High Street, W1U 4QW

Nearest station: Baker Street

Other locations: multiple, see website

dauntbooks.co.uk

83
DAUNT BOOKS
RICHARD OSMAN
LEGACY

BRITAIN
FIRE EXIT

REFERENCE
WRITING
WRITING

58

LASSCO

Reclaimed relics in elegant setting

Arranged across an immaculate Georgian mansion that doubles as a chic wedding venue, this stash of preloved gems is a million miles from your average antiques shop. It's got everything from Victorian boot jacks and Regency doorknobs to reclaimed Louis XV beds and moulded ceilings rescued from grand abodes. Stock varies wildly, but it's reliably fascinating – and consistently pricey. When you've finished hunting for heirlooms (or just a little inspiration), indulge your tastebuds at the on-site restaurant, where appropriately nostalgic dishes, from loaded devilled eggs to revamped rice pudding, are magicked up by renowned chef Jackson Boxer (grandson of cookbook legend Arabella, speaking of treasures).

30 Wandsworth Road, SW8 2LG
Nearest station: Vauxhall
lassco.co.uk

59

PENTREATH & HALL

Treasure trove of beautiful objects

Forget the 'I ♥ London' magnets and twee tins of tea bags; this bastion of Britishness stocks the only souvenirs worth smuggling home. Established in 2008 by designers Ben Pentreath and Bridie Hall, this small but generously stocked boutique never fails to intrigue with its ever-evolving edit of idiosyncratic treasures. Antique maps, commemorative crockery, London-centric globes and atmospheric English landscapes are just a handful of the mementos you'll uncover in this upscale Aladdin's cave, alongside collectable own-brand textiles and a selection of Hall's creations, from intaglio soaps to alphabet cups. Sign up for the weekly P&H email for inspiring blog posts and the first word on fresh drops.

57 Lamb's Conduit Street, WC1N 3NB
Nearest station: Russell Square
Other location: Rugby Street
pentreath-hall.com

60

TWENTYTWENTYONE

Iconic interior design store

Part of Islington's furniture for nearly three decades, this iconic design store stocks everything you could need to make a house a (profoundly tasteful) home. Specialising in 20th- and 21st-century furnishings (hence the name), twentytwentyone is your one-stop shop for timeless design classics, from hardwood-framed sofas by Robin Day to Enzo Mari-designed perpetual calendars and Eames dining chairs in every colour of the rainbow. In among the sofas, spotlights and side tables, you'll find high-end home accessories spanning Kay Bojesen wooden monkeys, Ole Flensted nursery mobiles and Louise Bourgeois placemats. Swing by for the latest vintage furniture acquisitions and ever-evolving home decor inspiration.

274–275 Upper Street, N1 2UA
Nearest station: Essex Road
twentytwentyone.com

61

LUNA & CURIOUS

Small but perfectly formed lifestyle emporium

Ok, so this self-styled 'miniature department store' isn't quite Harrod's, but its pair of treasure-stuffed rooms are just as browsable – and infinitely more tasteful. Established on Shoreditch's leafy Boundary Estate in 2006, this hip lifestyle favourite peddles everything from fashion-forward womenswear and joyful jewellery to robust kids' clothes, cherry-picked picture books and quirky homeware – all from sustainable indie brands such as Bobo Choses, Tiny Cottons and Bornn. Head here for keep-forever gifts for special kids and stylish friends – and inevitably end up treating yourself to something heirloom-worthy from the store's inventive own-brand label, magicked up by the trio of creative women at its helm.

24–26 Calvert Avenue, E2 7JP
Nearest station: Shoreditch High Street
lunaandcurious.com

Luna
&
CURIOUS

62

LABOUR & WAIT

Timeless basics

A name inspired by American poet Henry Wadsworth Longfellow feels fitting for a shop that radiates as much virtue as Labour & Wait. An early architect of Redchurch Street's renaissance, the oxymoronic 'luxury basics' store has been labouring in the area since 2000 (an epoch by Shoreditch standards), but could just as easily have been standing for a century – so intoxicating is its nostalgia. Inside, along with obliging staff in smart workaday aprons, you'll find everything from nifty camping stoves and posh picnic blankets to indestructible enamelware and natural feather dusters – all built to stand the test of time, both physically and aesthetically. Never has keeping your house in order felt so impossibly chic.

85 Redchurch Street, E2 7DJ
Nearest station: Shoreditch High Street
Other locations: Marylebone, Dover Street
labourandwait.co.uk

Chalk
Nails
JULY
NORTH AMERICAN MAMMALS
CAPTAIN SCOTT
UNDERSTANDING MAPS
THE STORY OF FLIGHT
UNDERWATER EXPLORATION
THE STORY OF TOOLS

85
LABOUR AND WAIT
GOODS
LABOUR
AND
WAIT
OPEN

63

AIDA

Sustainable shopping

AIDA could easily be just another oh-so-trendy Shoreditch boutique, but between its approachable staff, quirky homeware, laid-back cafe and the fact that it was named after the founders' nan, it manages to be a whole lot more. An enthusiastic champion of eco-friendly brands, the sustainable shopper's favourite offers everything from cult vegan trainers by VEJA to recycled homeware by Nkuku and organic cotton sweatpants from Colourful Standard. Come for high-quality tees and bum-flattering jeans you'll love forever – or just an idle browse around their excellent selection of smaller brands.

133 Shoreditch High Street, E1 6JE
Nearest station: Shoreditch High Street
aidashoreditch.co.uk

VEJA
LONDON IN LOCKDOWN
LONDON IN LOCKDOWN

64

IYOUALL

Nordic nesting

Why scrap with the hordes in flat-pack hell when you could opt for an infinitely more tranquil, tasteful (and totally meatball-free) Scandi-furniture-shopping experience? Set up in 2016 by Fleur Paterson and Matt Cottis of Dulwich design consultancy IYA Studio, iyouall is a Nordic furnishing fan's minimalist fantasy, showcasing everything from modular sofas to striking stationery from the cream of Scandi interiors brands (think HAY, Audo Copenhagen and String, to name a few). Come here for endless inspiration, envy-inspiring home accessories and goofproof gifts for sophisticated friends.

48 East Dulwich Road, SE22 9AX

Nearest station: East Dulwich

iyouall.com

LA HAINE

65

MEET BERNARD

A stylish encounter

We first met Bernard back in 2006, when Ryan and Dani Chandler opened their first menswear store in Greenwich and immediately began turning heads. Nearly two decades, a Covid closure and a foray into womenswear later, what is now southeast London's oldest independent fashion shop currently exists as a pair of tempting East Dulwich boutiques – one men's, one women's, both impossibly well curated with keep-forever treasures from Ganni, Howlin' and YMC, among copious other sustainable labels. If you've ever dreamt of digging through the wardrobes of the coolest guy and girl you know (and then stealing it all for yourself), this is your chance.

42 Lordship Lane, SE22 8HJ;
37 North Cross Road, SE22 9ET
Nearest station: East Dulwich
meetbernard.com

66

THE MERCANTILE

Immaculately curated womenswear

Old Spitalfields Market isn't quite the indie shopping haven it once was, but Debra McCann's (hence Mercantile) dinky boutique has remained a covetable constant, touting fashion-forward – but always wearable – clothing for the last 15 years. Playful and considered, the Mercantile edit is made up of more than 150 (largely sustainable) global brands, spanning high street favourites such as Nobody's Child and American Vintage through to cult labels including L.F. Markey and Flower Mountain. A godsend for women who want cool clothes but have better things to do than hunt them down.

17a Lamb Street, E1 6EA
Nearest station: Shoreditch High Street
themercantilelondon.com

saucony

67

COUVERTURE & THE GARBSTORE

Concept clothing store with indie focus

Husband-and-wife team Emily Dyson and Ian Paley have been keeping west London sharply clad for more than 15 years, tirelessly tracking down the world's most promising small and emerging designers and helpfully amassing their wares in their expansive Notting Hill boutique. This elegant three-storey townhouse is presented more like a home than a shop: head downstairs for Norse Projects chore jackets, Stüssy shirts and homegrown hoodies from Paley's Garbstore, or above deck for Cordera knitwear, Baserange lingerie and dreamy homeware and accessories from Dyson's female-focused (and supremely covetable) Couverture.

188 Kensington Park Road, W11 2ES
Nearest station: Ladbroke Grove
couvertureandthegarbstore.com

68

COAL DROPS YARD

Open-air shopping and dining

Formerly a hub of the coal industry, then a nucleus of the UK rave scene, this Victorian site was re-designed by Thomas Heatherwick in the mid-2010s. It's worth visiting for the undulating glass architecture and buzzy canal-side location alone, but stay to peruse the indie-heavy gaggle of boutiques and eateries that make your average food court look like feeding time at the zoo. Blomma Beauty's natural skincare, Cissy Wears' chic kidswear and Roseur's contemporary dried flowers are all must-visits. Once you've shopped, drop into Sons + Daughters for an epic egg-and-crisp sandwich, or alfresco cocktails and parrillas (Spanish DIY grills) at Barrafina off-shoot Parrillan.

Stable Street, N1C 4DQ
Nearest station: King's Cross St. Pancras
kingscross.co.uk

Shelter

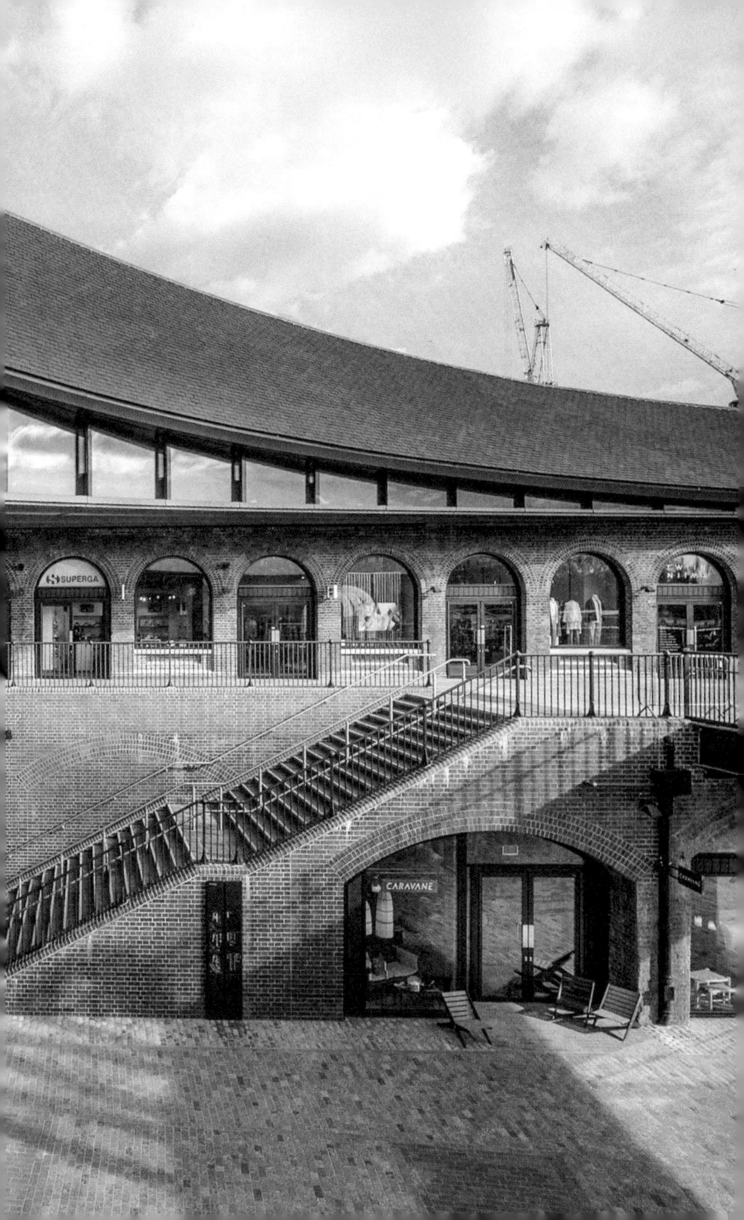
SUPERGA
CARAVANE

69

GOODHOOD

Indie lifestyle store

Life is good in the 'hood. At least, it certainly *looks* good. Skulking around east London since 2007, Goodhood appears either to have totally nailed the Shoreditch aesthetic or is largely responsible for it (and we suspect it's the latter). Multi-hued homeware, zeitgeisty wellness products, sweary dinner plates and rings chunky enough to inflict significant damage are just a few of the gems you'll discover in the third iteration of the cult lifestyle store, plus understated own-brand casualwear and a bunch of diverse collabs (with Dickies, Clarks, Origin Coffee, Stepney Workers Club et al.). If you're concerned you might be losing your cool, this place will restore it and then some.

15 Hanbury Street, E1 6QR
Nearest station: Shoreditch High Street
goodhoodstore.com

GOODHOOD
LONDON

70

COLUMBIA ROAD FLOWER MARKET

Blooming lovely Sunday pastime

Stroll down Columbia Road on a Sunday lunchtime and it might feel like the entire population of London has had the same idea. But while the jostling crowds, hawkers' cries and the intoxicating perfume of a thousand fresh blooms can trigger sensory overload, it's all part of the experience at this legendary East End flower market. Early birds catch the best buds, leaving themselves free to browse the street's 60 indie boutiques, bouquets in hand. Check out Lily Vanilli for seasonal sweet treats, Bob & Blossom for cute kidswear and VOUT for expertly selected vintage womenswear, before heading to The Nelson's for vegan roasts with a sassy soundtrack.

Columbia Road, E2 7RG
Nearest station: Hoxton
columbiaroad.info

TOP QUALITY'
EX-LARGE
DUTCH
TULIPS
TOP QUALITY
PEONY

71

CONSERVATORY ARCHIVES

Botanical paradise

The words 'garden centre' spectacularly undersell Conservatory Archives, a concept plant store for which 'untamed utopia' or 'rainforest portal' feel infinitely more apt. Unveiled in 2021, the store's Camden site is by far its most impressive, inhabiting a magical Victorian stable. Specimens err on the exotic, from the velvety-leafed *Philodendron melanochrysum* to white-flecked variegated monsteras and are arranged unsystematically to create the sense of ambling through a forest. And, while you won't find much in the way of gardening accessories here, the surprisingly inexpensive planters are top of the pots.

3 Middleton Mews, N7 9LT
Nearest station: Caledonian Road
Other location: Clapton
conservatoryarchives.co.uk

72

ARTIST RESIDENCE LONDON

Charmingly bohemian hotel

If you've got an aversion to soulless chain hotels, stay here instead. Occupying a characterful Regency townhouse in peaceful Pimlico, this delightfully eccentric hideaway promises an authentically *London* experience, with an eclectic vintage aesthetic. The best of the city is at your fingertips, from legendary landmarks at Westminster to pre-Raphaelite paintings at Tate Modern (no.31). Either side of the sightseeing, make time for lazy French toast in the chic restaurant, idiosyncratic cocktails in the cosy cellar bar and lingering soaks in your personal roll-top bath.

52 Cambridge Street, SW1V 4QQ
Nearest station: Victoria
artistresidence.co.uk

73

THE HOXTON

Boutique bolthole

Shoreditch might have lost some of its edge since the first guests checked into the Hoxton back in 2006, but this lively hotel remains a cult favourite. Cosy and convivial despite its industrial vibe, this boutique-on-a-budget mostly caters to style-conscious travellers but is just as beloved by the laptop-wielding freelancers that invariably fill its bare-brick lounge. Such capacious communal areas more than make up for the smaller sleeping quarters, which vary from a sizeable 'roomy' to a can't-swing-a-cat 'shoebox'. In fact, between zingy ceviche and inventive cocktails in the Peruvian rooftop restaurant and galvanising Bloody Marys and brunches in the all-day American diner, you might find yourself reconsidering the need to leave the premises at all.

81 Great Eastern Street, EC2A 3HU
Nearest station: Old Street
Other locations: Southwark,
Holborn, Shepherd's Bush
thehoxton.com

74

THE NED

Go big or go home

Everything about the Ned feels MASSIVE, from the palatial foyer (it used to be Midland Bank's headquarters) to the lavish Sunday buffet and the smiles on the faces of the preposterously helpful staff. Supposing your budget is equally sizeable – or you just want to experience the capital like a king – book yourself in for some Grade I-listed Art Deco opulence. You'll have access to the sumptuous spa and more swanky bars and restaurants than you'll have time to grace (try Millie's Lounge for top-notch afternoon tea or The Parlour for a decadent dinner with a side of cabaret). Or reserve a Heritage room and simply spend your stay luxuriating in your *gigantic* four-poster bed. Bliss.

27 Poultry, EC2R 8AJ
Nearest station: Bank
thened.com

75

BERMONDS LOCKE

Affordable aparthotel

Fancy living like a London Bridge local for a few days (or even up to a year)? Designed to shake up the traditional guesthouse experience, Locke's riverside aparthotel combines the convenience of a hotel with the privacy of an apartment, offering restful studios and suites complete with sofas and kitchenettes, all at very un-SE1 prices. If you want to be productive, there's a sunny coworking space downstairs, with caffeine boosts courtesy of the trendy in-house coffee bar and endless foodie options on the doorstep (Maltby Street Market and Bermondsey Street both so close you can almost smell them). On second thoughts, maybe we'll just stay forever...

157 Tower Bridge Road, SE1 3LW
Nearest station: London Bridge
lockeliving.com

13 12
SP
H1254
SF47E
BYW
23-10-19
A30 B
10 12

11 12
103E
BYW
18-12-19
19-09-19
FW139-H
55D
BYW

76

ONE HUNDRED SHOREDITCH

Sleek Shoreditch sanctuary

Its appellation refers to its door number rather than the emoji stamp of approval – although the latter would be just as apt. A glossy evolution of appropriately named predecessor the Ace Hotel, One Hundred is still every inch the hipster hangout, only the hipsters have grown up and they're craving a little more luxury. Taking its interior cues from Kubrick's *2001: A Space Odyssey*, this design-led haven lists sumptuous suites, a subterranean cocktail bar from master mixologist Mr Lyan, a rooftop bar with skyline views and a coffee bar brewing up blends from Origin (what else?) among its 100-plus reasons to make that reservation. (Insert 100 emoji here.)

100 Shoreditch High Street, E1 6JQ
Nearest station: Shoreditch High Street
onehundredshoreditch.com

77

SAGER + WILDE

Quintessential wine bar

Just the words Sager + Wilde should be enough to make anyone who's tried it tipsy with anticipation. For those who haven't, think old New York allure: worn bar stools, exposed brick and low lighting. Think cosy, candlelit evenings spent sampling by-the-glass 'unicorn' (sommelier speak for 'rare') wines poured from bottles with pretty labels by friendly (and never snooty) staff. Think modern spins on classic cocktails for those who don't do wine. Think soaking it all up with unpretentious bar snacks, from hunks of cheese on crackers to oozing doorstop toasties and unapologetically rustic charcuterie plates. Think perfect dates and rolling out the door at chuck-out time, woozy with joy.

193 Hackney Road, E2 8JL
Nearest station: Hoxton
sagerandwilde.com

78

CAFE OTO

Avant-garde music venue

This vibey venue has been broadening musical horizons since 2008, when co-founders Hamish Dunbar and Keiko Yamamoto took a chance on an abandoned paint factory in a still-edgy Dalston. Some 15 years on, the area has upped, come and priced out countless creatives, but Cafe OTO (which means 'sound' in Japanese) remains much the same, its intimate mood helped by its spartan (i.e. stage-less) aesthetic, with an emphasis on experimental new music above all else. Swing by after dark for everything from funk and jazz to noise rock and folk, or head down during the day for limited-edition books, records and hearty 'Persianesque' lunches, courtesy of resident chef Zardosht.

18–22 Ashwin Street, E8 3DL
Nearest station: Dalston Junction
cafeoto.co.uk

79

WILTON'S MUSIC HALL

Historic performance space

Keen on cabaret? Got a penchant for puppetry? Obsessed with opera? Whatever your cultural passion, stoke it at Wilton's, a Victorian grand music hall turned multi-arts performance space tucked behind Shadwell's historic Cable Street. Restored in the 2010s, this aged beauty still heaves with character – its crumbling plaster mouldings and peeling paintwork striking scars of its chequered past. For the ultimate East End music hall experience, arrive early for drinks in the atmospheric bar, before heading through to the barrel-vaulted auditorium for a Tom Carradine-led Cockney singalong around the piano. *Knees up Mother Browwwn...*

1 Graces Alley, E1 8JB
Nearest station: Tower Gateway
wiltons.org.uk

WILTONS
WILTONS

80

RIVOLI BALLROOM

Art Deco dance hall

Sure, nightclubs are fun. But don't you ever get the urge to whoop it up like your grand-parents used to? Step (or *chassé*) in Rivoli Ballroom, London's delightfully kitsch – and only surviving – 1950s dance hall, whose outrageous Art Deco interiors afford a suitably flamboyant backdrop to all your jitterbugging, hand-jiving, bunny-hopping escapades. And if you've two left feet (or if it's 1990s nostalgia you're here for), don't worry. As well as its inclusive ballroom dance bonanzas, the Rivoli regularly hosts laid-back club nights spanning everything from hip hop to house, as well as a pop-up cinema screening classic flicks under the barrel-vaulted ceiling. Vintage garb optional (but always encouraged).

350 Brockley Road, SE4 2BY
Nearest station: Crofton Park
rivoliballroom.com

81

THE AUDLEY

Art-infused mega pub

The Bentleys and Porsches that pull up periodically are the first sign that this pub is not like the others. The second is its richly adorned (now-listed) façade – designed by Thomas Verity of Lord's Cricket Ground Pavilion fame. But perhaps the most glaring indicator that The Audley is not your average boozer lies within its walls – specifically a kaleidoscopic, Phyllida Barlow-designed ceiling and the hypnotic Martin Creed neon that hangs above the bar (as well as plenty of other modern art, all thanks to its owners, the power duo behind gallery Hauser & Wirth). Get here early to secure one of the brown leather booths and something tasty from the joyfully London-themed menu. Pint of prawns and a Chelsea bun, anyone?

41–43 Mount Street, W1K 2RX
Nearest station: Bond Street
theaudleypublichouse.com

82

SKEHANS

Easygoing Irish pub

What makes a cracking pub? Or should that be a craic-ing pub? Indeed, this family-owned Irish indie, which regularly tops London's 'best boozer' lists, attributes much of its popularity to its sense of fun – something that appears to be the only common denominator among its diverse throng of punters. Whether you're here for the tense weekly pub quiz, near-nightly live music sets or just a quiet pint by the fire, there are always good times (and Guinness) on tap at Skehans.

1 Kitto Road, SE14 5TW
Nearest station: Nunhead
skehans.com

GUINNESS
BEER GARDEN
LIVE MUSIC
THAI FOOD

83

THE FALTERING FULLBACK

Backstreet boozer with a magical garden

There are roughly 4,000 pubs in London, but only one has a secret Ewok tree village hiding in its garden. This Finsbury Park favourite is a genuine Tardis, its ivy-cloaked veneer concealing an overgrown beer terrace over multiple levels. Begin your adventure in the front room's horseshoe bar (complete with vintage bicycles dangling from the ceiling) and then wind your way through the Alice-in-Wonderland-esque maze outside to find a spot amid the foliage for a pint and a plate of pad Thai.

19 Perth Road, N4 3HB
Nearest station: Finsbury Park
falteringfullback.com

FALTERING
FULLBACK
TO THE LAST

84

THE PELICAN

Grape-focused gastropub

This 150-year-old boozer has aged like a fine wine – its tasteful 2022 revamp rendering it one of the best places in west London to glug down a glass of... fine wine. Indeed, wine is a big deal at the Pelican, with seasonal selections and new bottles debuted each week, but there's plenty else to pile into your pouch here. Food is satisfyingly hearty, with modern spins on meaty classics and bar snacks (including mince on toast and gamey sausage rolls) dominating the menu – and the on-tap beers are *ale-right* too. Don't miss the monthly supper clubs and workshops, which are always worth poking your beak into.

45 All Saints Road, W11 1HE
Nearest station: Westbourne Park
thepelicanw11.com

DISPENSING
ENT.

85

LYANESS

Experimental cocktails in swanky surrounds

Forget piña coladas and Sex on the Beach – this audacious cocktail bar is much more likely to serve up something deliciously unexpected. Cricket-cordial suffused mezcals and petrified-poo martinis might sound like the sort of concoctions you'd resort to imbibing on a desert island, but this riverside spot is less castaway, more cruise liner with its plush teal banquettes and green marble bar (the latter a hand-me-down from owner Mr Lyan's Dandelyan, considered the best bar in the world before it closed). The drinks menu is fairly inscrutable but that's all part of the fun, and whether you plump for a refreshing Safety Frappé or a floral Doc Americano, you'll be far from disappointed.

20 Upper Ground, SE1 9PD
Nearest station: Blackfriars
lyaness.com

86

A BAR WITH SHAPES FOR A NAME

Modernist cocktails

Less is more at this enigmatic cocktail bar, whose philosophy is drawn from the simplicity of the Bauhaus movement – down to the primary-coloured two-dimensional shapes that stand in for any official designation on its frontage. Here, in hip mahogany surrounds, pithy cocktails are sold pre-packaged in hand-painted bottles. Or, if the combo you crave isn't available, staff dressed in bright boiler suits will mix it up from the deliberately modest bar. And while this all might sound a little pretentious, you won't care a jot once the impeccably designed tables are folded back onto the walls and you're gliding around the dancefloor guzzling on a lychee martini. Proof that names don't matter one bit.

232 Kingsland Road, E2 8AX
Nearest station: Haggerston
*instagram.com/a_bar_with_shapes_for_a_name_*

87

RIO CINEMA

People's picture house

In a city replete with faceless cinema chains, the Rio is a beacon of community-spirited indie joy. Entertaining Dalstonites for well over a century, this petite picture palace is legendary for its film clubs, which include classic matinees for over-55s in the Art Deco auditorium, queer films in the seductive Ludski Bar and arthouse-horror in the space-age basement screen. Worlds away from the extortion of Leicester Square, this not-for-profit is a staunch champion of accessible film for everyone, with cut-price tickets and resident discounts on selected days, as well as a parent-and-baby-club for culture-starved infant wranglers. Sign up as a 'friend' for special offers that will keep you on the edge of your seat.

107 Kingsland High Street, E8 2PB
Nearest station: Dalston Kingsland
riocinema.org.uk

RIO
RIO
CINEMA
GLORIA BELL
BOOK
DIEGO MARA DONA
WE ARE

88

BFI

Queen of the screens

If you think nothing beats seeing a film on the big screen, try the BFI IMAX – covering over 5,500 square feet – for size. Part of the institute's South Bank complex, this is the cinema to end all cinemas, showing new releases alongside cult classics, immersive documentaries and special-guest screenings in godly proportions. When the credits roll, take a short stroll over the subway to the riverside location, BFI Southbank, for a post-picture refuel in one of the buzzy bars; make it a movie marathon with another flick in one of three additional screens – with special seasons offering deep dives into niche genres or the work of particular directors; or take a trip down memory lane in the dazzling Mediatheque archive.

Belvedere Road, SE1 8XT
Nearest station: Waterloo
bfi.org.uk

BFI SOUTHBANK

89

DRUMSHEDS

Vast industrial nightclub

Anyone who endured the horror of the old Tottenham IKEA on a Saturday might baulk at the thought of spending another five hours in the same building – much less in the dark with 15,000 other people. Weirdly though, the site's latest incarnation is a rather more relaxing affair, despite (unofficially) being the biggest nightclub in the world. Indeed, in swapping hotdogs for house music and LACK shelving for lasers, this vast space appears to have found its true calling. Head here for the diverse line-up, friendly staff and daytime raves (kickout is at 10.30pm). And yes, those *are* the original IKEA escalators perfectly preserved at the entrance.

6 Glover Drive, N18 3HF
Nearest station: Meridian Water
drumshedslondon.com

90

MOTH CLUB

Fabled venue with eclectic programme

The cool crowd might flock to this ex-servicemen's club like a moth to the proverbial, but it's so much more than Hackney's hippest haunt. Taking its name from the Memorable Order of Tin Hats, an old military union that still meets at the venue, this much-loved establishment caters to an exceptionally diverse crowd, with weekly bingo nights, raucous stand-up, British Legion meets and seriously sweaty gigs on its eclectic line-up. The decor is wonderfully kitsch, with a gold glitter ceiling that makes this feel more like a school disco despite big-name acts, and the community spirit is palpable. One of London's *least* forgettable nights out, no matter how many reasonably priced drinks you've quaffed.

Valette Street, E9 6NU
Nearest station: Hackney Central
mothclub.co.uk

MOTH

IMAGE CREDITS

British Museum © Taran Wilkhu; Design Museum © Design Museum; Conservatory Archives © Rachael Smith; Columbia Road Flower Market © Chanel Irvine; Marksman © Helen Cathcart; The Pelican © The Pelican; Hampstead Heath © Nature Picture Library / Alamy; St. JOHN © Sam A. Harris; Chishuru © Harriet Langford, coutesy of Chishuru; Cadet © Sam A. Harris; Quo Vadis © Alexander Baxter; Camberwell Arms © Joe Howard; Pophams © Adrianna Giakoumis; *E5* Bakehouse © Sam A. Harris; Theo's © David Post; Mildred's © Mildred's London; Morito © Helen Cathcart; Akub © Matthew Hague; Sketch © Ed Dabney; Sessions Arts Club © Louise Long; Paul Rothe & Son, Beigel Bake, E. Pellici © Rachael Smith; Borough Market © Red Agency; The Drapers Arms © Orlando Gili; Rochelle Canteen © Helen Cathcart; Marksman © Tim George; Jolene © Philippa Langley; TOAD Bakery © Milly Kenny Ryder; Mamasons © Ola O Smit; BAO © Philippa Langley; Koya © Ola O Smit; Lyle's © Anton Rodriguez; Shakespeare's Globe © Commission Air / Alamy; British Museum © Taran Wilkhu; Southbank Centre © Paul Carstairs / Alamy; Tate Modern © Godrick; V&A © Peter Kelleher / V&A; Hampton Court first image © Escapetheofficejob / Alamy, second image © Nathaniel Noir / Alamy, third image © Steve Vidler / Alamy; Whitechapel Gallery © Guy Montagu-Pollock, courtesy Whitechapel Gallery; South London Gallery © Taran Wilkhu; National Portrait Gallery © Gareth Gardner; St. Paul's Cathedral © Taran Wilkhu; Somerset House © Botond Horvath / Alamy; Design Museum © Taran Wilkhu; Barbican Centre first image © Marco Kessler, second & third image © Taran Wilkhu; Hampstead Heath © Marco Kessler; Greenwich Park © The Royal Parks; Victoria Park © Martin Usborne; Kew Gardens © Marco Kessler; Primrose Hill © Joe Dunckley; Epping Forest © Marco Kessler; Battersea Park first image © Roger Cracknell / Alamy, second image © Martin Usborne, third image © Marco Kessler; Regent's Park © PhotoLondonUK; Hyde Park first image © Marco Kessler, second image © Ingus Kruklitis; Community Sauna Baths © David Post; GoBoat © Michael Pilkington; Castle Climbing Centre © PA Images / Alamy; Artwords © Charlotte Schreiber; Choosing Keeping © Lesley Lau; Present & Correct © Nick Dearden, courtesy of Architecture for London; Liberty © Tania Volosianko; Daunt Books first image © Rachael Smith, second image © Ellen Christina Hancock; Lassco, Pentreath & Hall, twentytwentyone © Lesley Lau; Luna & Curious © David Post; Labour & Wait © Lesley Lau; Aida © Chris Snook; iyouall © Tian Khee Siong; Meet Bernard © David Post; The Mercantile, Couverture & The Garbstore © Lesley Lau; Coal Drops Yard © Taran Wilkhu; Goodhood © David Post; Columbia Road Flower Market © Chris Lawrence / Alamy; Conservatory Archives © Rachael Smith; Artist Residence London © Artist Residence; The Hoxton © Toby Mitchell / The Hoxton; The Ned © The Ned; Bermonds Locke © Ed Dabney; One Hundred Shoreditch © One Hundred Shoreditch; Sager + Wilde © David Post; Cafe OTO © David Laskowski; Wilton's Music Hall first image © Taran Wilkhu, second image © Peter Dazeley, courtesy of Wilton's Music Hall; Rivoli Ballroom © Taran Wilkhu; The Audley © Helen Cathcart; Skehans, The Faltering Fullback © David Post; The Pelican © The Pelican; Lyaness © Roman Shabodalov; A Bar with Shapes for a Name © Remy Savage; Rio Cinema © Taran Wilkhu; BFI © Luke Hayes / BFI; Drumsheds © Luke Dyson; MOTH Club © Charlotte Schreiber

An Opinionated Guide to London
First edition

Published in 2024 by Hoxton Mini Press, London

Text by Emmy Watts
Editing by Florence Ward
Proofreading by Leona Crawford
Design support by Friederike Huber

With thanks to Matthew Young for initial series design.

Please note: we recommend checking the websites listed for each entry before you visit for the latest information on price, opening times and pre-booking requirements.

Thank you to all of the individuals and institutions who have provided images and arranged permissions. While every effort has been made to trace the present copyright holders we apologise in advance for any unintentional omission or error, and would be pleased to insert the appropriate acknowledgement in any subsequent edition.

A CIP catalogue record for this book is available from the British Library.

ISBN: 978-1-914314-74-2

Printed and bound by OZGraf, Poland

Hoxton Mini Press is an environmentally conscious publisher, committed to offsetting our carbon footprint. This book is 100 per cent carbon compensated, with offset purchased from Stand For Trees.

Every time you order from our website, we plant a tree:
www.hoxtonminipress.com

Selected opinionated guides in the series:

For more go to www.hoxtonminipress.com

INDEX